The Qur'an
An Eternal Challenge

al-Naba' al-Aẓīm

Muhammad Abdullah Draz

Translated and edited by
Adil Salahi

© **Cooperative Office for Islamic Propagation in Rabwah , 2019**
King Fahd National Library Cataloging-in-Publication Data

Osoul Global Center
   Al Naba Alazim. / Osoul Global Center . - Riyadh , 2019

   254 p ; 16 X 23 cm

   ISBN: 978-603-8229-74-3

   1-Quran - General studies   I-Title
   229 dc   1439/5741

L.D. no. 1439/5741
ISBN: 978-603-8229-74-3

Table of Contents

Contents	Page
Introduction	7
About the Book and Its Author	11
Postscript	17
Preface	21
Introduction	23
The Qur'an Its Definition and How It Differs from Hadith	27
The Source of The Qur'an	35
The Prophecies of the Qur'an	55
Muhammad's Teacher	79
A Source Beyond Man's Worl	95
The Qur'an: A Literary Miracle	107
The Secret of the Qur'anic Miracle	13
Surpassing Excellence in Every Passage	145
Broadest Meaning, Minimum Wording	165
The Unity of Each *Surah*	179
The Semantic Design of the Longest *Surah*	203

Introduction

The Qur'an was most fascinating to the Arabs when it was first revealed and recited to them. They were a nation that took great pride in its natural talent of beautiful expression. Numerous were their poets, despite the fact that they were largely unlettered. They rated fine expression as the top talent anyone could have. Therefore, a poet was given a high status in his tribe and he returned that favour by continuously singing his tribe's praises.

All this changed when the Qur'an was recited to them by Muhammad, the final messenger God sent to mankind. They recognised its great superiority to anything they had experienced. They realised that it was totally different from poetry, but they could not compare it to any style of expression they knew. It was enough to listen to one passage of the Qur'an for the chief of one of their largest tribes to comment: 'This is not the speech of any human being. Had it been human speech, we would have recognised it'.[1]

What makes the Qur'an so unique? Over the centuries, countless studies sought to answer this question. Some scholars came up with perceptive ideas, and others gave valid theories. Some wrote voluminous works, and others cited numerous examples to prove their theories. May God reward them all for their fine efforts.

1- Al-Mafrooq ibn Amr, the chief of the Shayban tribe, listened to the Prophet reciting verses 151-3 of Surah 6.

Introduction

The present work by Muhammad Abdullah Draz is a short one, but it ranks among the most preceptive studies of the style of the Qur'an. It sheds new light on its uniqueness and it reflects the depth of insight its author had. The author takes us into areas that are hardly touched upon by earlier scholars. The way that he shows the unity of each surah is particularly impressive.

The Osoul Center is proud to present this book to English readers. It hopes that it will enable them to better understand and appreciate the Qur'an, God's last message to all mankind.

Osoul Global Center

About the Book and Its Author

Introduction by Adil Salahi

> The word Qur'an in Arabic is a form of the infinitive, which means 'to read'. The term is used in this infinitive sense in the two verses: "It is for Us to gather it and to cause it to be read. Thus when We recite it, follow you its recitation." (75: 17-18). The term has come to acquire a new sense, which denotes the glorious Book revealed by God. Today, this is the most common usage of the word. It also occurs in God's statement: "This Qur'an shows the way to all that is most upright." (17: 9.)

Searching for sources for my essay, I went to a bookshop specialising in Islamic books. Here, I found a booklet on religion by Dr Draz which I included in my purchase for the day. However, the bookshop assistant recommended another book with the Arabic title *Al-Naba' Al-Aẓīm* as highly readable. I bought the book and started reading it that day. Interested in both Arabic literature and the Qur'an, I was hardly able to put the book down. I admired the author's style, for it is both fine and powerful. But the way he treated his subject matter was even more captivating. It was not particularly relevant to my essay, but it gave me, as every reader soon discovers, penetrating knowledge into the superior literary excellence of the Qur'an.

About 15 years later, I picked up another copy in London during a visit to a small Islamic bookshop. I read it again, and discovered that I learnt even more than during my first read of it. Dr Draz's scholarly treatment of his subject matter is such that the higher a reader's standard of education, the more he or she is able to benefit by it.

About the Book and Its Author

A few years ago, I attended a small study circle of one of my teachers, and he was reading a section of this book. The discussion that followed refreshed my mind of the priceless information it contains. That same evening I decided that the book should be made available in English. Soon afterwards, I started splitting the book into short articles which were published in my column, 'Islam in Perspective', in the Saudi paper, *Arab News*. Much of the book was published in this way. Now it has been completed, by God's grace, and it is my pride and pleasure to present it to English readers, providing as it does a rare insight into the Qur'an.

The author has one theme in mind throughout the book, which is to use the Qur'an itself to testify to its author, God Almighty. To this end, he uses the information provided in the Qur'an, which could not have been available to anyone but God, and he uses its style and method of expression. His analysis of the latter is masterly, showing a rare understanding of the text combined with a profound literary talent. Indeed, his own style combines power with simplicity. This makes the book a masterpiece with few peers in Qur'anic literary studies.

As I was finalising this work, I was so pleased to see a copy of Draz's other work, *Introduction to the Qur'an*. I have also learnt with great pleasure that efforts are underway to translate his work on Ethics and Morality in the Qur'an. This the author wrote in French as a thesis submitted to the Sorbonne for which he was awarded the degree of Ph.D. This translation will rely on the French original, as the author did not translate it himself.

Muhammad Abdullah Draz was born in 1894 in Mahallat Diyai, a village of Kafr al-Shaykh County in northern Egypt. His father was an Islamic scholar educated in Al-Azhar, the oldest university in the world. The father wanted his son to follow religious education, so he sent him to the religious institute of Alexandria, affiliated to Al-Azhar. He followed this religious line of education throughout his schooling, until he received his degree. He then decided to learn French, as he considered such knowledge of vital importance in serving the cause of Egyptian independence. During the popular uprising of 1919, he joined a number of young Egyptians visiting foreign embassies to explain the uprising and to seek help in persuading Great Britain, the colonial power, to accede to the demands of Egyptian people for independence. He also wrote in French defending Islam against its detractors.

In 1928, he was appointed to the teaching staff of the Department of Higher Education in Al-Azhar. He was then transferred, the following year, to the Department of Specialisation at the same university, and in 1930, he moved to the Faculty of *Uṣūl al-Dīn*, which specialises in the basic sources of Islamic knowledge.

In 1936, he was sent on a mission to France, where he stayed for 12 years. It was during this period that he was admitted to Sorbonne University and awarded his Ph.D.

On his return to Egypt, he taught the History of Religion at the University of Cairo, Qur'anic Commentary in *Dar al-ᶜUlūm*, a teachers' college which was, at the time, affiliated to Al-Azhar. He also taught Arabic and Moral Philosophy at Al-Azhar University. Furthermore, he was elected to the membership of Senior Islamic Scholars, i.e. *Jamāᶜat Kibār al-ᶜUlamā'* in 1949. He continued in these positions until his death in January 1958, when he was attending a conference in the city of Lahore, Pakistan.

In translating this work, I have tried to be faithful to the text. However, on a small number of occasions I have ventured to expand a little where I felt this to be necessary to make the point under discussion easier to understand. Where the author explains a point in a footnote, I have incorporated the footnote into the text, to ensure continuity and an easier grasp of the idea under discussion. However, where a footnote refers to something that is not immediately relevant to the text, I have left that as it is. On the other hand, I have omitted footnotes that are of a purely linguistic nature, because they would be very difficult for a non-Arabic speaking reader to follow.

About the Book and Its Author

As the book includes numerous Qur'anic references, I have relied mostly on Muhammad Asad's translation, *The Message of the Qur'an*, with slight alterations.

It was extremely difficult to choose a title for the English edition. In Arabic, the book is called *Al-Naba' Al-Aẓīm*, which means 'The Great News'. But the author chose this title as it is a Qur'anic phrase with clear connotations. However, he used it in a different context, making it refer to the Qur'an itself, while in Qur'anic usage, it refers to the Day of Judgement. An Arabic speaking reader who is familiar with the Qur'an will not have any problem with this change of usage, but how to find a title that provides a clear reference to the Qur'an and yet retains the element of topicality? After considering several alternatives and discussing them with friends, I had to give up the attempt. I felt it would be better to select a title indicating the subject matter of the book, without trying to retain the import of the original title. Hence the English edition has a totally different title.

Finally, I pray to God to shower His blessings on the author's soul and to make this effort complementary to his own in the service of the Islamic cause.

Adil Salahi

May 2001

Postscript

After the publication of the first edition of this translation, I met Mr Fathi Draz, the author's son, to present him with the English edition. We had a very interesting discussion about his father and his work. From him I learnt that it was before World War II that the author travelled to France to become the Director of the Central Mosque in Paris. At the time air travel was still in its early days while the majority of travel was by ship or by road. As the author was about to go on board his ship in Alexandria, a friend of his who came to bid him farewell asked him whether he intended to do a Ph. D. in France, he said that he hoped to do so. He further told him that he wanted to study the moral principles and values advocated by Islam.

After settling in Paris, Shaykh Draz put his application to enrol in the Sorbonne. Rather than do what every student in his situation would do, which is to enrol for a Master degree, as a first step to obtain a doctorate, Shaykh Draz applied to enrol as an undergraduate to study philosophy. Needless to say, this meant that this would delay his goal of graduating with a Ph. D. degree by four years. Explaining his reasons, Shaykh Draz said: 'I want to understand what the Europeans have in this area before I embark on my research'. He graduated with honours and then he started on his postgraduate study. His Ph. D. thesis was on the moral code the Qur'an lays down. His work was a large volume. His supervisor advised him that it was too large for a thesis, but he wanted him to complete the work, because he realised its

Postscript

superior value. When he completed his work, the university told him that it was too large and advised him to submit it as two theses, which he did.

On the day set for the examination of his thesis, his external examiner greeted him warmly. The discussion took a totally unusual turn. His external examiner said to him: 'I have a few questions to ask, but I would like you to understand that I am not questioning or objecting to anything you have written, I am asking in order to learn'. This work was translated into Arabic by Dr Abd al-Saboor Shaheen.

Adil Salahi

April 2017

Preface

This book is both new and old. Its latter parts are new, while its early chapters are old. Its inception took place on a university campus, over 20 years ago, but only its head, neck and chest had appeared then. As for its limbs and final shape, these have only been completed today.

Students of the old days witnessed its beginning, when parts of it were dictated to them at varying intervals. Whenever they had gathered something like 20 pages, or even less, they would print them and urge the author to add the remaining chapters. However, circumstances at the time did not allow that it should be so completed. The parts that were already printed were left with those students. Today, however, God has willed that the author should add new material to complete this work, so as to take it out of the narrow environs of academic life to the broader stage of publication. This makes it an address to every person with a critical mind, to everyone who takes or rejects matters only on the basis of evidence. Its appeal is made to the intellect that seeks practical proof of what is presented.

This discourse begins at the very beginning. It requires no prior commitment or conviction from its reader, nor does it need any prior cultural perception or educational qualification. It only appeals to the reader to start with no prior prejudice, to be equipped with a keen desire to determine the truth concerning the Qur'an. This will ensure that he knows the truth of the Qur'an, by God's will.

March 1957
Muhammad Abdullah Draz

Introduction

> Praise be to God who has favoured us above all other communities by sending us the Qur'an, the like of which He has not given to any other community. He has made the Qur'an a book of guidance for all mankind in all times, and a final version of all Divine messages. He has also placed within it irrefutable and timeless evidence testifying to its truth. Peace and blessings may be showered on the Prophet Muhammad whose manners and behaviour were a practical implementation of the Qur'an, and who has made the Qur'an the subject of his will and the sum of his heritage. It is he who says: "The best of you is one who learns the Qur'an and teaches it to others".

Our Lord, as You have blessed me with a share of the Qur'an which you have described as a 'wise reminder,' enabling me to learn and memorise it and enriching my mind with the love of its recitation and understanding, I pray to You to place me among those who adhere to the guidance it provides, who are ready to defend it, and those who will be resurrected on the Day of Judgement under its banner. These are the supporters of our great leader, the noblest of all God's Messengers, Muhammad ibn ᶜAbdullāh, peace be on him, his household, companions and followers.

This book is a study of the Qur'an which I introduced in my course 'Commentary on the Qur'an', taken by students of Al-Azhar Mosque and University. My objective in undertaking this piece of research has been to describe the Qur'an by its true qualities and colours, to present some facts

Introduction

concerning the Qur'an and to chart the course to be followed in studying it. In most chapters I have tried to adopt an analytical approach, speaking in detail and adding some examples. I have not limited myself to indicating something where I am able to explain it in full. My hope is that it will help those who have so far been neglectful of the Qur'an to open their minds and hearts to it, so that they will find its light spreading rapidly before them. I also hope that believers will find in it what strengthens them in their faith.

Our Lord, perfect for us the light You have given us, and forgive us. Indeed You have power over all things, and You answer the prayers of Your servants.

Muhammad Abdullah Draz

Chapter 1

The Qur'an

Its **Definition** and How It Differs from **Hadith**

The word Qur'an in Arabic is a form of the infinitive, which means 'to read'. The term is used in this infinitive sense in the two verses: *"It is for Us to gather it and to cause it to be read. Thus when We recite it, follow you its recitation."* (75: 17-18). The term has come to acquire a new sense, which denotes the glorious Book revealed by God. Today, this is the most common usage of the word. It also occurs in God's statement: *"This Qur'an shows the way to all that is most upright."* (17: 9.)

In fact, it is called 'The Qur'an' because it is actually read by mouth, and it is called 'The Book' because it is written down with pens. Both names are derived from what actually takes place with regard to it. The fact that these two descriptions have come to be treated as names of the Divine Book refers to its rightful treatment which requires that it be kept and preserved in two places instead of one: people's memories and the pages of a book. Thus, should an error find its way into one, the other will correct it. We do not trust what a reciter learns by heart unless it is confirmed by the written text which has been unanimously approved by the Prophet's companions and which has come down to us, through the generations, in its original form. Nor do we trust the writings of any scribe unless it is confirmed by what scholars who memorise the Qur'an have shown to be its correct version through uninterrupted chains of reporters.

This double care, which God has ensured, imparts to the Muslim community a keen desire to keep the Qur'an intact, in conscious following of

The Qur'an

the Prophet Muhammad's guidance. This exceptional care has ensured that the Qur'an remains in an unassailable position with regard to its accuracy and purity from all distortion. This is a practical aspect of the fulfilment of God's promise to preserve the Qur'an in its original form, as it is clear in His statement: "*It is We Ourselves who have bestowed from on high this reminder, and it is We who shall truly preserve it [from all corruption].*" (15: 9.) Hence, it has remained free from all manner of distortion, corruption and interruption of reporting which befell earlier Scriptures. Those Scriptures God did not take upon Himself to preserve. He left it to people to guard and keep. He says: "*And so did the [early] men of God and the rabbis, inasmuch as some of God's writ had been entrusted to their care; and they all bore witness to its truth.*" (5: 44.) This distinction has a reason. All former Divine revelations have been meant to apply for a period of time, not for all times. The Qur'an, on the other hand, was sent down from on high to confirm the truth of what was revealed earlier and to supersede them all. Thus, it contains all that they established of true fact, adding whatever God has willed by way of addition. It takes over their roles, but none of them may play its role. It is God's will that the Qur'an should remain the final arbiter until the Day of Judgement. When God wills something, He, Wise and All-Knowing as He certainly is, brings together what ensures that His will is done as He pleases.

In this fine sense, the Qur'an may be described as particular and true, as may be said in logic. Hence, it is difficult to define it by any standard logical definition which speaks of kinds, parts and characteristics. This applies to all that is true and particular: they cannot be defined in this manner, because each part of a logical definition is universal in itself, and what is universal cannot, conceptually, be exactly like what is particular. This is because the universal applies to all that is mentally considered identical to it in that sense, even though it may not exist in reality. Thus, it does not distinguish it from everything else. As such, it does not become a truly definitive description.

A particular object is defined by reference to it when it is physically present or familiar to our minds. Thus, if you want a definitive description of the Qur'an, you have no way of doing so unless you refer to it as it is written down in its book or read by mouth. You will then say: "it is what is contained between this front cover and this back cover." Or you may say: "It is the following text – [and then you read it all from the first word in Surah *al-Fātiḥah*, or The Opening, to the last word in Surah *al-Nās*, or Men.]"

The definitions used by scholars in terms of kinds and parts, which are normally used to define universal facts, are mainly intended to make it easier to understand and to distinguish it from whatever may be given a similar name, even falsely. All books revealed by God, sacred hadiths and some of the Prophet's hadiths are, like the Qur'an, revelations by God. Someone may, on the basis of this fact, imagine that these may also be called by the same name, the Qur'an. Hence, scholars try to explain that the name applies only to it by highlighting its qualities and characteristics that distinguish it from all others. They may define the Qur'an as follows: "The Qur'an is the word of God, which He has sent down to Muhammad [peace be on him] and the recitation of which is a form of worship."

When we analyse this definition we find that the term 'the word' refers to a type that includes all speech, but when it is attributed to God, it excludes the speech of everyone else, human, *jinn* or angels.

That this word of God is 'sent down' excludes all other words of God that He has kept to Himself or addressed to the angels to implement without imparting it to any human being. Not every word of God has been revealed or sent down. Indeed, what has been sent down is only a small portion: *"If all the sea were ink for my Lord's words, the sea would indeed be exhausted before my Lord's words are exhausted, even though We were to add to it sea upon sea."* (18: 109.) *"If all the trees on earth were pens, and the sea were ink, with seven more seas yet added to it, the words of God would not be exhausted."* (31: 27.)

The definition makes a further exclusion by saying that it is 'sent down to Muhammad.' This excludes what has been sent down to earlier prophets, such as the Torah revealed to Moses and the Gospel revealed to Jesus, and the Psalms revealed to David and the scrolls sent down to Abraham [peace be on them all] .

The last exclusion is indicated by the phrase which describes its recitation as a form of worship. This means that the Qur'an includes only the part of revelation that we are ordered to read in prayer and at other times as part of our worship. Thus, everything that we are not required to recite is excluded, such as the methods of recitation which have been transmitted by single reporters at a time, unlike the methods of recitation transmitted by large numbers of reporters in every generation. Also excluded are the sacred hadiths, which quote God Himself, if we take the view that their wording was revealed by God.

Ordinary hadiths said by the Prophet may be divided into two categories according to their meanings: the first is 'deduced', which includes those hadiths the Prophet stated on the basis of his understanding of God's word or his contemplation of the universe. This category is certainly not part of the word of God. The second category is 'received.' The import of such hadiths is given to the Prophet through revelation and he has taught it to mankind in his own words. This means that in meaning and content, this second category is attributed to God, but in its phraseology should be attributed to the Prophet [peace be on him]. Normally speech is attributed to the speaker who constructs it in its style, even though the meaning it expresses may be one that is very familiar and has been transmitted from one person to another. Thus, the two categories of hadith are excluded because the first qualification in the definition of the Qur'an is that it is 'God's word.'

Similarly excluded is the sacred, or *qudsi* hadith, if we say that it is revealed in meaning only. This is the weightier view in our judgement. Had it been revealed in wording as well, it would have had the same sanctity as the Qur'an. There would be no grounds for distinguishing two types of revealed speech attributed to God. Had the case been so and the *qudsi* hadith been revealed in word and meaning, it would have been imperative to preserve it intact, and it would not be permissible to quote it in meaning only, and its narrator would not have been allowed to handle its sheets without performing ablution. No scholar has ever claimed that.

In addition to the fact that we are required to implement the Qur'an in practice, it also has another purpose, which is to set a challenge by its superior style and to perform worship by its recitation. Hence, it had to be revealed by word and text. The *qudsi* hadith has no such additional purposes of challenge and worship. It is simply revealed for the implementation of its message. For this purpose, understanding the meaning is sufficient. To claim that it is revealed in word as well is to claim what is unnecessary and without a solid basis, except perhaps the phrases mentioned in some of the *qudsi hadiths* attributing the statement to God. But what we have already said tells us that this applies to the meaning rather than to the wording. It is, in fact, common usage in Arabic. When one explains a line of poetry, for example, one says, 'the poet says so and so', and when we explain in our own words a verse of the Qur'an we say, 'God tells us this and that'. In the same way God tells us what Moses, Pharaoh and others said, stating the import of what they actually said, but expressing it in words and styles other than those they used. He nevertheless attributes those words to them.

If we were to claim that nothing other than the meaning is sacred in a *qudsi* hadith, we would be right to use the same description, i.e. *qudsi*, in reference to some of the Prophet's hadiths as well, because they include meanings revealed by God. The answer to this is that we know for certain that a *qudsi* hadith has been revealed in meaning. We have clear statements by the Prophet which attribute it to God Himself. In this it is distinguished from ordinary hadiths which have no such attribution. Thus, it is possible that an ordinary hadith may be taught to the Prophet by revelation or deduced by him through reflection. Hence we describe all hadiths as statements by the Prophet, because this is what we are certain of. Had we had a distinctive mark to indicate the part that is revealed to the Prophet, we would have called it *qudsi* or sacred as well.

The Qur'an

However the division of hadith into these categories does not entail any practical distinction. We must act on every hadith, whatever its category is. The Prophet is honest and truthful in what he conveys of what is revealed to him and he is always right in what he deduces. He is also supported by the Holy Spirit, who does not allow a mistake to pass, should the Prophet make any such mistake in matters of religion. This means that in both respects, what the Prophet says has its origin in what is revealed to him, either by instruction or by confirmation. Hence, we must accept all his *Sunnah* and act on it, as we are commanded in the Qur'an: *"Take whatever the Prophet gives you and refrain from whatever he forbids you."* (59: 7.) *"Whenever God and His Messenger have decided a matter, it is not for a believing man or a believing woman to claim freedom of choice insofar as they themselves are concerned."* (33: 36.)

Chapter 2

The Source of The Qur'an:

Divine Text, Divine Meaning

It is universally known, beyond any shred of doubt, that this sublime book, the Qur'an, was delivered to mankind through Muhammad ibn ʿAbdullāh ibn ʿAbd al-Muṭṭalib (peace be on him), an unlettered Arab man born in Makkah in the sixth century. This much is not subject to disagreement between believers and non-believers. No other book or event in history is so universally accepted as such.

Now the question arises: was Muhammad ibn ʿAbdullāh (peace be upon him) its author, expressing his own thoughts? Or was it given to him by a tutor? If so, who might that tutor have been?

We read in this very book that it is not the composition of the man who brought it to us. It is described as: *"The word of a noble and mighty Messenger, who enjoys a secure position with the Lord of the Throne. He is obeyed in heaven, faithful to his trust."* (81: 19-21) This Messenger is Gabriel, the angel, who received it from God, the Wise, the All-Knowing. He then brought it down in a clear and lucid Arabic style and conveyed it to Muhammad. Muhammad (peace be upon him) received it from him as a student receives a text from his teacher. What he did with it after he received it was: 1) to learn and memorise it; 2) to report and convey it; 3) to explain it; and 4) to implement it in practical life. He had nothing to do with the creation of its meanings or the setting of its purpose. It is all an inspiration which was revealed to him.

2. The Source of The Qur'an

There are numerous references to this fact in the Qur'an itself, such as: *"When you [O Prophet] do not produce any miracle for them, they will say, 'Why do you not seek to have one?' Say: 'I only follow whatever is being revealed to me by my Lord.'"* (7: 203.) *"Say: It is not for me to alter it [i.e. the Qur'an] of my own volition; I only follow what is revealed to me."* (10: 15.) There are many other texts that refer to the revelation of the meanings of the Qur'an. We also have references to its being revealed by word as well: *"We have sent it down from on high as a discourse in the Arabic tongue."* (12: 2.) *"We shall teach you to read, and you shall not forget."* (87: 6.) *"Do not move your tongue in haste [repeating the words of the revelations], for it is for Us to gather it and to cause it to be read. Thus when We recite it, follow you its recitation. Then it is for Us to make its meaning clear."* (75: 16-19.) The Prophet is given instructions such as 'read, convey, recite,' all in connection with the Qur'an and its verses. All these, as well as 'moving his tongue' and the text being in Arabic apply to the wording and the text, not to its meanings.

The Qur'an states very clearly and unequivocally that neither Muhammad (peace be upon him) nor any other creature had anything to do with the composition of the Qur'an. It was revealed by God, in word and meaning.

It is very peculiar that some people still require evidence to prove the first part of this question, which is that Muhammad did not write it himself. Had this been a case looked into by any judge whose sole aim is to establish the truth, the judge would have done no more than to accept this testimony by Muhammad himself. He would not have required any further evidence, material or logical. There is no claim being made here to require irrefutable evidence. It is an admission that is binding on the one who makes it. Neither friend nor foe would hesitate to accept it from him. No rational person who makes a claim to leadership and supports his claim with miraculous events would attribute his finer goods to someone else, disowning them totally and completely. In fact, the opposite is true: his position would be enhanced if he were to claim such goods for himself. Moreover, he would meet no objection to his claim from any person on earth.

What we know is that many writers resort to plagiarism in order to claim for themselves what other people have written. Or they plagiarise what gives their writings some finer qualities when they feel that their action is unlikely to be detected. In fact, some of them resort to grave digging, in order to claim for themselves stuff written by authors that have been long dead. No one in history has ever attributed to someone else the finest pieces of his own thought, or his most superb writings, or the most precious jewel in his crown. This is unheard of. If we were to suppose that this could happen, we cannot find any reasonable or even semi-reasonable justification for it.

A naïve person may suggest, however, that such an aspirant to leadership might have thought that by attributing the Qur'an to Divine revelation he may find it easier to win people's obedience for his orders. Such a claim, it might be thought, would give his orders a special sanctity which could not otherwise belong to them had he declared that he himself had issued them all. But this is false, both in essence and in nature.

It is essentially false because the man who brought the Qur'an to us made statements that he attributes to himself, and others that he attributes to God Almighty. What he claims to be his own is no less binding on us than what he attributes to God. Nor is obedience of the latter more imperative. In fact, he claims the same degree of obedience for both types without distinction. Their sanctity is the same. To obey him is to obey God, and to disobey him is to disobey the Almighty. If it is a question of obedience that is behind the claim of Divine authorship, then why has he not claimed it for everything he himself said?

This is also false in nature because it relies on an unfounded assumption that such a leader is one who wishes to establish reforms, but who does not mind giving his reforms a foundation of lies and falsehood. Historical truth disproves this. Anyone who monitors his conduct in all that he says and does, explicit or implicit, in situations of pleasure or anger, in private and in public, can only conclude that no one could be further from cunning or deviousness. In fact, he was always very truthful and accurate, in small and serious matters, whether alone or with others. This was the most pronounced and clearest of his characteristics, both before and after prophethood. In fact, both his friends and enemies testified to this, in his own lifetime and up to our present day. *"Say: Had God so willed, I would not have conveyed this [Qur'an] to you, nor would He have brought it to your knowledge. Indeed, a whole lifetime have I dwelt among you before this [revelation came to me]. Will you, then, not use your reason?"* (10: 16.)

It may be useful to give here some very clear examples from the Prophet's own conduct which testify to his truthfulness in stating that the Qur'an is God's revelation and that he could not have produced any part of it on his own initiative. Sometimes he went through hard times which required some statement to be made. In fact, the need was so urgent that had the matter been left to him, he would have found the words to say and the occasion to make such a pronouncement. But days and nights went by and he would not find any Qur'anic statement to recite to people concerning the emergency he was facing.

The hypocrites in Madinah fabricated their false accusations of adultery concerning his wife, ᶜĀ'ishah. Nothing was revealed to him concerning this for a while. Time passed and people continued to talk, and those affected were in utter distress. He, himself, had to be so reserved in what he said about his wife: "I have seen nothing evil from her." He did his best to investigate the matter and consulted his trusted companions. A whole month passed by, and everyone said that they knew her to be of good and honest character. At last he could say to her nothing more than this: "ᶜĀ'ishah, I have heard this and that being said about you. If you are innocent, then God will make your innocence clear. If you have done something wrong, then seek God's forgiveness."

These are his own words as he could view the matter. We realise that this is the statement of a human being who has no knowledge beyond what his faculties of perception give him, and one who would not make a conclusion without firm evidence, and would not say what he does not know to be true. But he hardly uttered these words when the opening part of Surah 24, 'Light', was revealed to him declaring her complete innocence, and giving a clear verdict of her purity and faithfulness. [The relevant hadith is related by Al-Bukhari, Muslim and others.]

Had the matter been up to him, what would have prevented him from producing such a verdict earlier to protect his own honour and his own wife. He could have attributed that verdict to Divine revelation in order to silence those who continued to spread such rumours. However, Muhammad, a man who had never lied to other mortals, would not lie to God: *"Had he dared to attribute [falsely] some sayings to Us, We would indeed have seized him by his right hand, and would indeed have cut his life-vein, and none of you could have saved him."* (69: 44-47.)

There were times when the revelation he received ran contrary to what he preferred. It might declare his view to be wrong, or permit him something to which he was disinclined. Had he delayed acting on it for a short while, he would have been strongly reproached and criticised, even though it might have been a matter of little consequence. Several examples may be quoted here:

- *"Prophet, why do you impose on yourself a prohibition of something that God has made lawful to you, only to please your wives?"* (66: 1.)

- *"You would hide within yourself something that God was sure to bring to light, fearing [what] people [may think], whereas it is God alone whom you should fear."* (33: 37.)

- *"May God pardon you, [Prophet]! Why have you granted them permission [to stay at home] before you come to realise who was speaking the truth and before you come to know the liars."* (9: 43.)

- *"It does not behove the Prophet and the believers to pray for the forgiveness of those who associated partners with God, even though they happened to be their near of kin, after it has been made clear to them that they are destined for hell."* (9: 113.)

- *"But to the one who considered himself self-sufficient you were all attention. Yet the fault would not be yours if he remained uncleansed. As to him who comes to you with zeal and with a feeling of fear in his heart - him you ignore and busy yourself with trifles."* (80: 5-10.)

Let us reflect on these verses and the reproach they contain. Had they been the expression of Muhammad's remorse and feelings of guilt and sorrow, when he realised his mistakes, would he have spoken about himself in such a strongly reproachful manner? Would he not have preferred to keep quiet in order to maintain respect for his own views and orders? Indeed, had the Qur'an been the product of his own conscience, he would have suppressed some parts of it when the need arose. And had he wished to suppress any part of it, then such verses would be the first to be so suppressed. But the Qur'an is God's own revelation, and Muhammad could not suppress any part of it: *"He does not begrudge others the secrets of what is unseen."* (81: 24.)

Consider very carefully the following verses from Surah 8, 'The Spoils of War', and you will find something very peculiar about the case to which they refer:

> *"It does not behove a prophet to take captives unless he has battled strenuously and shed blood on earth. You may desire the fleeting gains of this world, but God desires [for you] the life to come. God is Almighty, Wise. Had it not been for a decree from God that had already gone forth, there would indeed have befallen you a tremendous punishment on account of what you have taken. Enjoy, then, what you have gained as lawful and good, and remain conscious of God. God is indeed much-forgiving, merciful."* (8: 67-69.)

These verses were revealed only after the captives in the Battle of Badr were released and ransom was accepted from them. They start with a denunciation of this action as wrong, and conclude with approving it and consoling the Prophet and his companions. Indeed this precedent, which earned reproach, became the rule to be applied in similar cases. Had this statement been made by Muhammad himself, is it conceivable that the psychological condition which produced its beginning could produce its conclusion, without any period of time to intervene between the initial rebuke and remonstration, and the ultimate approval? Certainly not. If we were to imagine that these two thoughts followed each other within any one person's soul, the latter would have cancelled the former altogether. The final thought would have approved what was actually done. What would be the reason, then, for describing the thought that was cancelled and erased and recording it in such a way that implied public rebuke? Why would the gain that was described as lawful and good be shown first to be at least undesirable? What psychologists understand from this text is that there are two entirely separate beings, one of them a Master saying to His servant, "You have done badly, but I pardon you and permit you to benefit by what you have done."

If you examine these errors for which the Prophet is reproached, you are bound to conclude that they share a common denominator. When the Prophet had to choose between two options, and found that neither involved anything prohibited, he would always choose what was more compassionate, more likely to win over his people to accept God's guidance, or to soften the hostility of his opponents. He would always choose the option that was less harsh and unlikely to raise doubts about Divine faith. At no time with regard to these incidents did he have a clear text which he wilfully disobeyed or forgetfully breached. All that he did was to consider and reflect. When he felt that he had a choice, he chose the option closer to his kind heart. All that can be said in such cases is that he exercised his discretion and made a choice. Let us suppose that his choice was mistaken; would he not, in this case, be justified, worthy of reward? The option he chose was the best that anyone endowed with human wisdom would have chosen. The Qur'an only draws his attention to what is better according to Divine wisdom. Do we find in this any reasonable error that requires rebuke and reproach? Is it not a question of God speaking to His beloved servant, and taking him up the road of finer education?

The Source of The Qur'an

ᶜAbdullāh ibn Ubay, the leader of the hypocrites, died and the Prophet gave his family his own robe to wrap him in for burial. He also wanted to perform the *janāzah* prayer[1] for him and to pray for his forgiveness. ᶜUmar objected to this saying to the Prophet, "Are you to pray for him when your Lord has forbidden you that?" The Prophet (peace be upon him) said: "He has not forbidden me, but has given me a choice, saying, '*Pray that God may forgive them, or do not pray for their forgiveness. If you were to pray seventy times that they be forgiven, God will not forgive them.*' (9: 80.) I will pray for him more than seventy times." And so he did. But God later revealed to him: "*Never shall you pray over any of them that has died, and never shall you stand by his grave.*" (9: 84.) The Prophet then stopped praying for any of the hypocrites.

Read this story, which is highly authentic as it is related in the two *Ṣaḥīḥ*, or authentic hadith anthologies, of al-Bukhari and Muslim, and reflect on it. What does it reveal to you, other than a picture of a servant of God who has taken the Qur'an as a course of action, studying its text to decide what steps to take? It also shows you a very kind-hearted person who feels that the first verse gives him a choice between two options, and he immediately chooses the one that is full of kindness and grace. He does not resort to the other course of action until he receives a clear order. Whenever you study the Prophet's attitude in such cases or in others, you will find the two elements combined: complete submission to God and exceptional kindness that knows no limit. By contrast, the Qur'an gives the attitude that shows strength untampered by motives and purposes. It provides a clear verdict, one which distinguishes between truth and falsehood, whether people like it or not. It is the strength that remains unaffected by people's attitudes, whether they believe or not. It is neither increased by people's obedience, nor weakened by their disobedience. We can, thus, realise what gap lies between the two. It is certainly a great gulf that separates master and servant, worshipped and worshipper.

1- The prayer that should be offered for a deceased person shortly before burial.

Sometimes he, the Prophet, received a statement expressed in general terms, or an order that sounded highly problematic. Neither he nor his companions could find a clear interpretation of it until an explanation was given to him at a later time. Should we not ask here: what rational human being inspires himself with words that he himself does not understand, or gives himself an order without recognising its purpose? Do we not find in this clear evidence that he is not the initiator, but simply the bearer, of a message, and that he does not issue orders, but receives them?

A verse was revealed stating: *"Whether you bring into the open what is in your minds or conceal it, God will call you to account for it."* (2: 284.) The Prophet's companions were very disturbed by this, and felt it to constitute a very heavy burden, i.e. they thought that they would be called upon to account for every fleeting thought. They said to the Prophet: "Messenger of God, this verse has been revealed and we feel it to be too hard to bear." He said: "Do you want to say like the people of former Scriptures said, 'We hear and we disobey'? Say instead, 'We hear and we obey. Our Lord, grant us Your forgiveness.'" They continued to say this supplication until God gave them its explanation in a subsequent verse that states: *"God does not charge a soul with more than it can bear. It shall be rewarded for whatever good it does and shall be responsible for whatever evil it does. Our Lord, do not take us to task if we forget or err. Our Lord, do not lay upon us a burden such as You laid on those before us. Our Lord, do not burden us with what we do not have the strength to bear. Pardon us and forgive us our sins, and bestow Your mercy on us. You are our Lord Supreme: grant us victory against the unbelievers."* (2: 286.) When this verse was revealed, they realised that they are held to account only for what they can bear of thoughts and feelings. This means that people are accountable only for what they resolve to do and take steps to fulfil, not for fleeting thoughts and hopes that are entertained without any choice.

The hadith that relates all this is authentic as it is given in full by Muslim and others, while Al-Bukhari refers to it in brief. The point here is that the Prophet did not know the interpretation of the verse to start with. Had he known it, he would have explained it to his companions when they raised their questions. He would not have suppressed such needed information, leaving his companions in a state of real anxiety, especially when he was well known for his care, kindness and compassion. He was in the same position as they, waiting for its interpretation to be revealed to him. God in His wisdom chose to delay that interpretation for a while. Similarly, He, in His wisdom, included the particle 'then', which indicates delay in His statement: *"When We recite it [i.e. the Qur'an], follow you its recitation [with all your mind]. Then it will be for Us to make its meaning clear."* (75: 18-19.)

Read, if you will, the account of the dispute at al-Hudaibiyah in al-Bukhari's *Ṣaḥīḥ* and in other authentic collections of hadith. For here you will find some hard evidence further substantiating our argument.

God had given permission to the believers to fight anyone who initiated any aggression against them wherever they might be, provided that they fought in the Haram only someone who attacked them there in person. He says in the Qur'an: *"Fight for the cause of God those who fight against you, but do not commit aggression. God does not love aggressors. Slay them wherever you may come upon them, and drive them away from wherever they drove you away; for oppression is even worse than killing. But do not fight them near the Sacred House of Worship unless they fight you there first. Should they fight you, then kill them. Thus shall the unbelievers be rewarded. But if they desist, then God is much-forgiving, merciful."* (2: 190-192.)

Therefore, when the Prophet's companions decided to visit the Sacred House that year, i.e. year 6 A.H., they took their arms with them as a precaution against attack. They only did this so as to defend themselves against possible aggression. When they were near the Haram area, they heard that the Quraysh, the major Arabian tribe which lived in Makkah and fiercely opposed Islam, had resolved to prevent them, mobilising its forces nearby. They, however, were not alarmed, because they were ready to fight in self-defence. In fact, they were more determined to complete their journey to the Mosque. Should they be prevented by force, they would meet force with force. The Quraysh was not in fighting shape after having suffered several setbacks. This meant that all motives to fight a decisive battle against a weakened enemy were there. The truth of Islam was certain to triumph and the falsehood of paganism would be wiped out.

When the Muslims were at Al-Hudaibiyah, the Prophet's she-camel, which was known by the name al-Qaṣwā', sat down, refusing to continue the journey. His companions tried hard to make her stand up and proceed, but she would not respond. They said, "She has become mulish." The Prophet said, "She has not become mulish, for mulishness is not in her character. She has been prevented by the same cause which prevented the elephant from continuing its march." What he meant was that God, who caused the Abyssinian army aiming to destroy the Kaʿbah and the elephant marching at its head to halt, now held the Prophet's she-camel back thus stopping the Muslim army from entering Makkah by force. He, thus, realised that God had not sanctioned their forceful entry into Makkah that year, be they the ones to start the use of force, or the ones to repel it when it was used against them by the Makkans. He, therefore, poked the she-camel and she moved to another position. He then encamped at the far end of al-Hudaibiyah. He stopped his march in response to this sign from God. Yet he was unaware of the wisdom behind His actions.

The Prophet then tried to enter Makkah by making peace with the Quraysh. He said: "By Him who holds my soul in his hand, I will grant them any proposal they make, provided it honours what God has sanctified." But the Quraysh refused him entry by peace or war. They went even further, imposing very hard conditions, requiring him to go back that year, and to return anyone from Makkah who would try to convert to Islam, while the Quraysh would not return to him anyone from Madinah who reverted to pagan beliefs. These were conditions that could never have been imposed by the Quraysh in its state of weakness against the much stronger Muslims. Nonetheless, the Prophet ordered his companions to release themselves from consecration, without completing their *umrah,* and to return to Madinah.

We need not ask about the dismay this peace agreement caused in the ranks of the Prophet's companions. When they shaved each other's heads, some of them, in their sad state almost accidentally cut their brethren's necks with their blades. Some of them were terribly shaken. They questioned one another, and some talked to the Prophet personally, asking him, "Why should we accept humiliation on account of our faith?" Thus, the army was close to a mutinous mood, and control could have been lost.

Suppose that the commander of that army was the one who made the plan, or participated in its making, or even realised its wisdom. Would it not have been his natural attitude to explain to his lieutenants the objectives he reckoned would be achieved as a result, instead of letting matters remain on the boil? But what was the Prophet's reply when ʿUmar questioned him about the wisdom of the agreement? He simply said to him: "I am God's servant and Messenger. I shall not disobey Him and He will never abandon me." In other words, he stated that he was only a servant of God, carrying out His orders. But he was at the same time confident of victory, whether it came straightaway or took a while.

As they marched on their return journey to Madinah, the Prophet's companions were still unaware of the wisdom of the settlement the Prophet had accepted. Then Surah 48 of the Qur'an, entitled Victory, was revealed to explain it all, telling them what profound wisdom dictated such agreement, and what God had in store for them. With this clarification, they realised that what they initially thought to be a sell-out was indeed a great victory. Little do human beings appreciate God's wisdom and His planning. The surah tells the Muslims:

> *He it is who, in the valley of Makkah, stayed their hands from you and your hands from them, after He had enabled you to vanquish them; and God saw what you were doing. It was they who disbelieved and who debarred you from the Inviolable House of Worship and prevented your offering from reaching its destination. And had it not been for the believing men and women [in Makkah], whom you might*

have unwittingly trampled underfoot, and on whose account you might have become guilty, without knowing it, of a grievous wrong. In time God might admit to His grace whomever He wills. Had they been clearly discernible [to you], We would indeed have imposed grievous suffering on such of them as were disbelievers. Whereas the disbelievers harboured a stubborn disdain in their hearts - the stubborn disdain born of ignorance - God bestowed from on high His gift of inner peace upon His Messenger and the believers, and bound them to the spirit of God-consciousness: for they were most worthy of this [Divine gift], and deserved it well. And God has full knowledge of all things. Indeed, God has shown the truth in His Messenger's true vision: most certainly shall you enter the Inviolable House of Worship, if God so wills, in full security, with your heads shaved or your hair cut short, without any fear. He has always known what you yourselves could not know. And He has ordained [for you] besides this a victory soon to come." (48: 25 - 27.)

Al-Zuhri, an early Muslim scholar of the generation that followed the Prophet's companions, says: "No preceding victory in the history of Islam was greater than al-Hudaibiyah. Those were victories achieved after fighting. When the truce was made and peace was achieved, people feared nothing from one another. They met and made contacts and talked with one another. No one with any degree of sound reason who was approached about accepting Islam could reject it. Indeed, in the two years following the peace of al-Hudaibiyah, the Muslims more than doubled in number." Another scholar comments: "As a result of the peace and security that prevailed after the agreement, people of the two sides were able to mix freely, without being subjected to reproach. Many of those who believed in Islam in secret were able to publicise the fact. Muslims were keen to recite the Qur'an to unbelievers and argued with them in peace. Prior to that, unbelievers could only talk to Muslims in secret. The whole affair was one of disappointment to the unbelievers, the while they thought it would bring them a moral victory."

The Source of The Qur'an

At the beginning of his message, the Prophet used to receive Qur'anic revelations with a keen desire to commit them to memory. He used to vocalise what was revealed to him with a movement of tongue and lips for fear that he might forget parts of it. This was not known as a habit of his whenever he prepared what he wanted to say, neither before nor after prophethood. Nor was it a characteristic of the Arabs. They only prepared their speech mentally. Had the Qur'an been a product of his own making, he would have followed the same pattern he and his people used in preparing their speeches. He would have thought about it more deeply and carefully, in silent concentration. This would have been more conducive to the production of sound opinion and well thought-out ideas. But he did not do this because he found himself suddenly being taught something that was given to him without preparation. Neither reflection nor deep thinking would have brought it to him, even had he sought it. Nor could he manage to facilitate a reminder, should he forget any of it. Nevertheless he was required to recite it accurately, word for word. In the face of this new requirement, which he was not used to, he felt he needed to follow the process of revelation very carefully. He continued to do so until God guaranteed him that he would memorise it and convey it accurately. *"Do not move your tongue in haste, [repeating the words of the revelation], for it is for Us to gather it and to cause it to be read. Thus when We recite it, follow its recitation. Then it is for Us to make its meaning clear."* (75: 16 19.) *"Do not approach the Qur'an in haste, before it has been revealed to you in full, but always say: 'My Lord, cause me to grow in knowledge.'"* (20: 114.)

These are some glimpses of the Prophet's attitude towards the Qur'an. They all confirm his assertion that the Qur'an did not emanate from himself, but was rather given to him. It was not his thinking that produced it, it was bestowed from on high.

When we consider his action and behaviour, we are bound to admire his refined manners and the great values to which he constantly adhered. We find in him a man of unblemished purity and complete seriousness. His tongue would not utter a word without knowledge, and his eyes would not attempt to conceal anything different from what he declared. Moreover, he would not listen to those who were wont on exaggeration as they sang his praises. He was great in his humility, with frankness and honesty that are very rare among leaders and with meticulousness that is exceptional even among scholars. How can such a person indulge in deception or fraud? How can he allow arrogance to creep into his character? Far be it from him to do so. A few further examples may be useful here.

A few maids were playing the tambourine in the morning after the wedding oalAr-Rubayyi ᶜ bint Muᶜawwidh of the Anṣār. They commemorated their fathers who were martyrs in the Battle of Badr. One of them sang: "And among us is a Prophet who knows what will take place tomorrow." The Prophet said to her: "Do not say that, but go back to what you were saying earlier." [Related by al-Bukhari.] This is confirmation of what God says in the Qur'an: *"Say: I do not say to you that God's treasures are with me, nor do I say that I know what lies beyond the reach of human perception."* (6: 50.) *"Say: It is not within my power to bring benefit to, or avert harm from, myself, except as God may please. And if I knew that which lies beyond the reach of human perception, I would have attained good fortune in abundance."* (7: 188.)

On the day when Makkah fell to Islam, ᶜAbdullāh ibn Abi al-Sarḥ was among a few people whom the Prophet stipulated were to be barred from any pardon, because of their unwavering hostility towards Islam and their harsh enmity towards the Muslims. When this man came to the Prophet with ᶜUthmān who pleaded his case, the Prophet was slow to accept his declared repentance. He delayed any acceptance of it until the man had repeated it three times. When he had left, the Prophet said to his companions who attended him: "Could not a wise one among you have killed the man when you saw me holding my hand from accepting his pledge?" They said: "How could we have known what you wished? You might have given us a signal with your eye." The Prophet said: "It does not behove a Prophet to have a treacherous eye." [Related by Abu Dāwūd and al-Nasā'i].

The Source of The Qur'an

A young boy of the Anṣār died and his body was brought to the mosque for prayer. ᶜĀ'ishah said: "Blessed is the abode of this one. He did not do anything sinful." The Prophet said to her: "You should not say this, ᶜĀ'ishah. God has created heaven and created those who deserve it, and created it for them, even before they were conceived. He has also created hell for those who deserve it, even before they were conceived." [Related by Muslim and others.] Scholars say that what is stated here took place long before the Prophet came to know that Muslims who die in childhood go to heaven.

When ᶜUthmān ibn Maẓᶜūn died, a woman from the Anṣār called Umm al-ᶜAlā' said: "May God bestow His mercy on you, Abu al-Sā'ib. I bear witness that God has given you an honourable position." The Prophet said: "How do you know that God has given him a position of honour?" She said: "To whom would God give a position of honour, then?" He said: "As for him, he has seen the truth, and I sincerely hope that he is well treated. By God, even in my position as God's Messenger, I do not know what will be done with me." She said: "By God, I will never again praise anyone." [Related by al-Bukhari and al-Nasā'i]. This is confirmed by the verse: "*Say: I am not the first of God's Messengers; and I do not know what will be done with me or with you, for I am nothing but a plain warner*". (45: 9.) Scholars explain that this was before the revelation of the opening verses of Surah 48, Victory, in which God tells him: "*God will grant you His forgiveness of all your faults, past as well as future.*"

If anyone thinks that he steered away from telling lies as a wise precaution, so that nothing happened in the future to show him to have resorted to saying an untruth, what could have prevented him from saying whatever he wished about what happens after death? He would have feared no objection or opposition from anyone. Nor would there be any future judgement on what he said. What prevented him, however, was his great character which understood his accountability to a Judge who is far superior than history and historians: "*We shall most certainly call to account all those to whom a Divine message was sent, and We shall most certainly call to account the messengers themselves, and thereupon We shall most certainly reveal to them Our knowledge [of their doings]: for never have We been absent from them."* (7: 6-7.)

Try, if you will, to remove any sense of certainty from your mind, allow yourself a maximum degree of doubt, and admit even the worst suspicions in any single event of the Prophet's noble life. Once you have examined a reasonable number of events you will inevitably find yourself unable to resist certainty unless you suspect your own mind and conscience. Critics study the life of a poet through his poetry, forming a complete picture of his beliefs, habits, manners, line of thinking and lifestyle. The fine images he includes in his poetry will not stop them from discerning the reality behind all the imagery. The truth has an overpowering force, one which shines through screens and curtains to reveal itself between the lines. Hard as he may try to conceal his real personality, a human being will inevitably allow a slip or an oversight in what he says or does, which shows his natural reaction when he finds himself under pressure, or in an embarrassing situation, or in a position of need, or when he is too confident. It is as the Arab poet says: "Whichever characteristic a person has will certainly come out, even though he may think himself able to conceal it."

Taking this into account, what can we say about the Prophet's life that gives us in every event and episode a clear picture of his pure self. It shows us complete harmony between inner feelings and outward appearances, as well as absolute honesty and sincerity in every word he says and every action he does. Indeed, a discerning person would see his great moral standards and refined manners in his face, even before he said or did anything. Hence, many of those who were inclined to accept Islam, as the Prophet called on them to do, did not ask him for evidence to support what he said. Some of them were close friends or relatives who knew him well, while others were complete strangers who recognised his honesty as they looked into his face. ʿAbdullāh ibn Sallām reports: "When God's Messenger arrived in Madinah, people gathered to see him, and everyone was saying, 'God's Messenger has arrived!' I also came to look at him. When I looked attentively at the face of God's Messenger, (peace be upon him), I realised that his face was certainly not the face of a liar."

Now that we have related these examples, we restate our purpose which is to show that a person of such fine character, and with such humility regarding the Qur'an, could never have been suspected of telling an untruth when he declared that he was not the author of that Book, and that his position in relation to it was that of a student who wanted to learn. In fact, this admission should be taken as another evidence of his humility and candid character.

Chapter 3

The Prophecies of the Qur'an

> The question of the Prophet having nothing to do with the writing of the Qur'an is too self evident to need any verbal admission from him or a study of his morality. It is definitely sufficient to prove a person's innocence of a particular action of commission that his very nature shows his physical inability to do or produce it. Let us now reflect on whether Muhammad, the unlettered Prophet, could have produced the Qur'anic concepts and meanings on the basis of his own knowledge and intellectual means.

Atheists, who have no shortage of ignorance, will claim that he could. They would argue that his innate intelligence and penetrating insight enabled him to distinguish right from falsehood, decent moral values from foul ones, and good from evil. They would even go further and claim that if there was anything in the heavens which could be grasped by deep reflection or sound nature or inspiration, Muhammad would have grasped it, given his undistorted nature, great intellect and profound abilities for reflection.

We believe that his qualities and characteristics are far more splendid than what such atheists credit him with, but we wish to ask: Is everything in the Qur'an deducible by reflection and contemplation, or is it something that one can feel and experience? Certainly not. We find in the Qur'an a substantial portion that can never be gathered by simple intelligence or contemplation, profound as they may be. No one who was not present at the time when historical events took place could have full knowledge of them except

3. The Prophecies of the Qur'an

through study and learning. What can such atheist people tell us about what the Qur'an relates of the history of former nations and the accurate details it gives of such events? Can history ever be formulated through deep thinking or accurate insight? Or would they go as far as to claim that Muhammad lived among those communities of former times, moving among them, and witnessing these events as they took place? Or had he studied the books of former authors so deeply that he learnt every little detail in them?

They cannot make either claim, because they, as well as the whole world, realise that neither situation applies to Muhammad, (peace be upon him), *"You were not with them when they drew lots as to which of them should be Mary's guardian."* (3: 44.) *"You were not with them [i.e. Joseph's brothers] when they resolved upon what they were going to do and wove their schemes [against him]."* (12: 102.) *"You were not on the sunset slope [of Mount Sinai] when We imposed the Law upon Moses, nor were you among those who witnessed [his times]."* (28: 44.) *"You have never been able to recite any Divine book before this one [was revealed], nor did you ever transcribe one with your own hand - or else, they who try to disprove the truth of your revelation may indeed have had cause to doubt it."* (29: 48.) *"These accounts of something that was beyond the reach of your perception We now reveal to you, [Muhammad], for neither you nor your people knew them fully before this."* (11: 49.) *"In the measure that We reveal this Qur'an to you, We explain it to you in the best possible way, seeing that before this [i.e. the Qur'an] you were indeed among those who are unaware of what revelation is."* (12: 3.)

We do not say that no one among the Arabs had ever known the names of some past prophets or past communities, or had a general idea of the destruction that overwhelmed the peoples of ᶜĀd and Thamūd or the great floods at the time of Noah. Such general notions rarely ever remain unknown to any person wherever he lives, in desert or city. They constitute part of human heritage and are the basis of many a proverb in different languages. The important part is that which concerns minute details only available in well-researched books, giving accurate accounts. Such knowledge was totally unavailable to the Arabs who were largely an illiterate people. It was known only to a handful of scholars. Yet you find accurate accounts of such history in the Qur'an. Even figures correspond perfectly. In the story of Noah, as related in the Qur'an, he is said to have lived among his people for a thousand years less fifty. And in the Book of Genesis we read that he lived nine hundred and fifty years. The People of the Cave are reported in the books of the Jews and the Christians to have remained in their cave for three hundred Gregorian years. In the Qur'an, they are mentioned to have stayed "three hundred years add nine." These nine account for the difference between Gregorian and lunar years. Consider this accurate arithmetic in a community of illiterate people who did not write or calculate.

It is certainly an amazing story. Here is an unlettered man who lives in a community of unlettered people, attending their gatherings, as long as they are free of falsehood and frivolity, leading a normal life, earning his family's living, working as a paid shepherd or merchant. He has no contact with scholars of any type. He lives in such circumstances for more than 40 years. Then all of a sudden he comes up with statements the like of which he has never uttered in the past, nor mentioned to anyone before. He says about communities of older times what could only be gathered from books treasured by scholars. Is it in such matters that those ignorant non-believers claim that he made a rational conclusion or gathered an inspiration? What logic supports the claim that this newly observed stage was a natural outcome of the preceding illiterate stage?

There is no escaping the rational conclusion that this sudden transformation was the result of some totally different cause that should be sought away from the limitation of his own soul or the sort of scanty information that was available to him. The atheist Arabs of the days of *ignorance* were more logical in their explanation of this phenomenon and had a better understanding of this secret than latter day atheists. Those Arabs did not say that he invented these stories out of personal inspiration. What they claimed was that he must have received knowledge that was not available to him previously, and that he studied such knowledge thoroughly in order to learn what he had not known: *"Thus do We give many facets to Our revelations. And thus they may say, 'You have learnt it well.'"* (6: 105.) *"They say: Fables of the ancient times which he has caused to be written down, so that they might be read out to him at morn and evening."* (25: 5.)

They certainly tell the truth. He has studied it well, but at the hand of his teacher, the Holy Spirit. He has caused it to be written down, but from *"honoured pages, exalted, purified, by the hands of noble and devout scribes."* (80: 13-16.) *"Say: Had God willed it otherwise, I would not have conveyed this [revelation] to you, nor would He have brought it to your knowledge. Indeed a whole lifetime have I dwelt among you before this [revelation came to me]. Will you not, then, use your reason."* (10: 16.)

That is what we have to say about the historical information contained in the Qur'an. It could only have come from a source outside Muhammad's own mind and soul. As for other types of information given in the Qur'an, the claim may be made that it could have been gathered by an intelligent person through deep reflection or sudden inspiration. Such an argument may appear logical to start with, but it soon collapses as a result of thorough examination.

The human mind has a special route through which to grasp ideas, thoughts or concepts. It also has a certain limit that it cannot exceed. Anything that does not fall directly within our normal senses or inner faculties of perception, and which has no roots within the human instinct can only be understood through an appropriate premise that leads to what has not been known. This can be either suddenly as in surmise or intuition, or slowly as in deduction and construction. Whatever is not introduced through one of these ways cannot be grasped by the human mind in any other way. It has only one remaining source, namely, inspiration, or quoting someone who has received such inspiration.

Now let us look at non-historical information given in the Qur'an. Do we find any means and introductions given for them in order that the human mind is able to grasp them? We will answer this question presently, but we will now give two examples of such meanings. The first belongs to religious beliefs and the other to unknown prophesies.

Concerning religion, the maximum that the human mind can gather through independent thinking, and with the help of undistorted human nature, is to realise that this universe is controlled by a powerful and mighty God. God has not created this universe in vain, but has established it on the basis of wisdom and justice. Hence, it must be returned a second time to give everyone his just reward for whatever he did of good or evil deeds. This is all that a perfect human mind may gather concerning religion.

But the Qur'an does not stop at this. It explains the limits of faith with considerable detail, describing the beginning and the end of creation, heaven and its bliss and happiness, hell and its varieties of suffering, as though we see both with our eyes. It tells us even the number of the doors of hell and the number of angels that guard these doors. On what rational theory are such figures and exact details given? This information is not something the human mind can produce on its own. It may either be false, which means that it is a wild guess, or true, which means that it has been taught by someone with accurate knowledge. But it is certainly the truth confirmed by books revealed earlier, and believed unhesitatingly by their followers: *"We have made their [i.e. the angels guarding hell] number nothing but a trial for the disbelievers, to the end that they who have been granted revelation aforetime might be convinced, and that they who have believed may grow yet more firm in their faith."* (74: 31.) *"Thus We have revealed to you, [Muhammad], a life-giving message, at Our behest. Prior to it, you did not know what revelation is, nor what faith implies."* (42: 52) *"No knowledge would I have had of what passed on high when they argued."* (38: 69.) *"This Qur'an could not have been devised by anyone other than God. It certainly confirms the truth of whatever remains [of earlier revelations] and clearly spells out the Book, revealed without doubt by the Lord of all the worlds."* (10: 37.)

The Prophecies of the Qur'an

Now let us consider how a perfect mind deals with prophesies of matters unknown. It can only rely on its past experience, making it a light that may predict a few steps along the course of future events. In other words, it makes that which is known and already experienced a criterion by which to judge what is to come. Its judgement is always taken very cautiously, saying: "This is what may be deduced if matters are to follow their natural course, and provided that nothing out of the ordinary takes place." Making a firm prediction, with definite details, even in matters that are not indicated by a scientific premise or an informed guess, is done only by one of two types of person. The first is a person who does not care what people say about him, or whether they describe him as a liar. This is the behaviour of fortune tellers. The other type is a person that has a covenant with God, and God does not breach a covenant He makes with anyone. This is the behaviour of prophets and messengers sent by God. No one else makes such predictions except one who quotes from either of these two types.

So to what category belongs the carrier of the Qur'an when he gives us a definitive statement outlining what is to happen in a year's time or after a few years, or what happens in the rest of time, or what will never take place at any time? He has indeed given us such predictions in the Qur'an, yet he never before made any attempt to give any information about the future, nor did he ever claim any knowledge of astrology or fortune telling. He was never given to making any such wild claims as such people do. What he gave us in the way of revelation was totally different from theirs. Fortune tellers and astrologers may give a mixture of what is true and what is false. He, on the other hand, disclaimed any knowledge of the future and never aspired to gain such knowledge. Yet it came to him naturally. Whatever he told of it has never been disproved. Indeed, no subsequent circumstances were ever able to disprove a single letter of what he foretold: "*It is indeed a sublime Book. No falsehood can ever attain to it openly, nor in a stealthy manner, since it is bestowed from on high by One who is truly wise, ever to be praised.*" (41: 41-42.)

We will give some examples of the prophesies given in the Qur'an, explaining some of their historical circumstances. We will then consider whether there were any premises leading to them available at the time so as to make such prophesies the product of deep contemplation coupled with excellent intelligence. We will confine ourselves to three types of prophesies. The first relates to prophesies concerning the future of Islam itself, or as represented by the Qur'an and the Prophet, while the other two concern prophesies in relation to the future of the two parties: that of God and that of the Devil.

Certainty of the Future

Examples of the first type relate to the religion of Islam and that God has ensured that it will remain forever, and will never be wiped out. These also include the promise that God will preserve the Qur'an intact, free from distortion. Verses giving these promises are in plenty, such as: *"Thus does God depict truth and falsehood. The scum is cast away, but that which is of benefit to mankind remains on earth."* (13: 17.) *"Do you not see how God compares a good word to a good tree? Its root is firm and its branches are in the sky. It yields its fruits in every season by leave of its Lord."* (14: 24.) *"It is We that have revealed this Reminder, and it is We Ourself that shall preserve it."* (15: 9.)

Do we know when such happy news, and indeed firm promises, were issued? All these verses were revealed in Makkah, and we all know the difficulties Islam went through in its early period in that city. It went through ten years of hostility, when the people there were not prepared even to listen to the Qur'an. Indeed, they prevented others from listening to it. The small number of believers who followed Muhammad were subjected to much pressure and persecution. Then, the Prophet's whole clan were boycotted and besieged in their quarters for a long period of time. Furthermore, there were secret, and even open, conspiracies to assassinate the Prophet or to send him into exile. Would anyone detect in the thickness of such endless darkness, any faint ray of hope which might have brought those persecuted people a

The Prophecies of the Qur'an

chance to proclaim their faith and to call publicly on others to follow it? If a reformer entertains such a hope, it is based on what he himself feels about the nature of his message. It certainly does not rely on the apparent course of events. Would he, in such circumstances, allow the hopes he entertains to grow so strong as to become an absolute verdict?

Suppose that he is so optimistic and hopeful that he is convinced that his message will triumph in his own lifetime, as he is giving it all that he can. How will he guarantee that his message will survive after his death, in the midst of overpowering future events? How can he be so certain when he knows that every lesson in history shows that there can be no foundation for such certainty? Many a reformer pursues a clear message of reform, but soon his call dies down. Cities have flourished in history, but have then declined and now we see only their ruins. Prophets were killed, and holy books were lost, destroyed or distorted.

Was Muhammad ever a man to entertain high hopes or allow his aspirations to control his action? Before he began to receive revelations, he never entertained any hope that he would be a prophet: *"You never hoped that this Book would be revealed to you. Yet it is only through your Lord's mercy that you have received it."* (28: 86.) Even after he was chosen as a Prophet, he could not guarantee that his revelations would remain with him: *"If We pleased We could take away that which We revealed to you: then you should find none to plead with Us on your behalf. But your Lord is Merciful to you. The grace He has bestowed on you is great indeed."* (17: 86-87.)

Such a guarantee to preserve the Qur'an intact must, by necessity, come from an external source, not from within himself. Who could give such a guarantee over an extended future, knowing that time brings a new surprise every day? Who could guarantee that except the Lord that controls time and conducts all events, the One who determines the beginning and the end of everything that takes place in the universe and who controls its course? If it were not for God's grace and mercy which He promised him in the verses quoted above, the Qur'an would not be able to stand firm in the face of the determined fight against it that we still witness from time to time.

Refer to history, if you will, to find out how often it turned against Muslim states. How often the enemies of Islam were able to overcome the Muslims and kill large numbers of them indiscriminately. Indeed, they forced whole Muslim communities to deny Islam and to follow other faiths. They burned books and destroyed mosques. Indeed, only a few of the atrocities they perpetrated would have ensured that the Qur'an would have been totally or partially lost, as happened to earlier sacred books. It is only through God's grace that the Qur'an has remained intact despite all the determined efforts of its enemies to destroy it. Its verses continue to be read as they were originally revealed, and its rulings still apply and continue to be implemented. We may look into daily newspapers to find out what great financial resources are used every year to obliterate the Qur'an, or to turn people away from Islam through falsehood, deception and temptation. But those who stand behind such efforts and supervise the spending of all these resources gain nothing except what God has spelled out in the Qur'an: *"The unbelievers expend their riches in debarring others from God's path. They will continue to spend their wealth in this way, but they shall rue it, and in the end they will be defeated."* (8: 36.)

The fact is that the power that ensures that the Qur'an will never cease to exist is the same One that ensures that the heavens and the earth will not fall and break away. Indeed it is God who *"has sent forth His Messenger with guidance and the true faith to make it triumphant over all religions, however much the idolaters may dislike it."* (9: 36 & 61: 9.) God will certainly accomplish His purpose, and perfect His light, ensuring that it will continue to spread and illuminate people's hearts and the world at large. Hence the Qur'an will continue to enjoy its overpowering position, unaffected by the hostility of anyone until God's purpose is accomplished.

A Challenge to All Mankind

A further example is the challenge to all creation to produce anything that resembles the Qur'an at any time: *"Say: If all mankind and the jinn* combined to write the like of this Qur'an, they would surely fail to come up with anything like it, even though they would all join efforts to do so." (17: 88.) "If you doubt what We have revealed from on high to Our servant, produce even one surah comparable to this Book. Call on your witnesses to help you, if what you say be true. But if you fail, as you will certainly fail,..." (2: 24.)

Consider this absolute and categorical statement. Can any Arab who knows what he is talking about give such a verdict when he knows that literary excellence was a major pursuit of the Arabs, and competition in that field was open to all? [It should be added here that although the Arabs did not read and write, they had natural literary gifts of the highest calibre, reflected mainly in their poetry which continues to be studied as model of literary excellence.]

Everyone knows that a critic can carefully study what an earlier writer has produced and then be able to find in it something that the original writer missed out or overlooked. He then improves on it or adds to its beauty. When the Prophet put this challenge to them, did he not consider that he would risk a great literary confrontation with a community that enjoyed native literary gifts in abundance? What could he do if a group of them commanding proven literary talents joined forces to come up with a text that excelled the Qur'an, or at least matched it in some aspects? This would involve one of them writing something with which to pick up the challenge, then all of them trying to improve on it, as they often did with poetry. Could he risk the possibility that such an effort could meet the challenge he put to them?

Moreover, if he felt that he could get away with such a challenge in his own generation, how could he make the same verdict applicable to all future generations, right up to the Day of Judgement, and to mankind and the *jinn* alike? That is indeed a risk no one in his right mind would take unless he was fully certain of what fate would bring about, and be assured of it by none other than God. He threw the challenge out to all the world, and it was like a judgement that applied to all and sundry. No one ever tried to come up with anything similar to the Qur'an without his attempt ending in miserable failure.

Guaranteed Protection

A third example is found in the verse in which God guarantees to protect His Messenger and assures him of his safety until he has completed his task of conveying God's message: *"O you Messenger of God! Proclaim what is revealed to you from your Lord. If you do not, you will then have failed to convey His message. God will protect you from all people."* (5: 67.)

Such a guarantee cannot be claimed by any human being, not even by a king who is well screened, and with a military cordon protecting him wherever he goes. How often have kings and rulers been assassinated, even when they were in a procession, surrounded by guards and soldiers? Consider, then, how literally the Prophet took this true promise. Al-Tirmidhi and Al-Ḥākim relate on the authority of ʿĀ'ishah, the Prophet's wife, and al-Ṭabarāni relates on the authority of Abu Saʿīd Al-Khudri that "the Prophet used to have guards at night. When this verse was revealed, he dismissed his guards saying to them, 'You may go home, for God has given me His protection.'"

God indeed protected him from his enemies in many situations when death was so close and when only God's protection could have saved him. One of these events is reported by both Ibn Ḥibbān and Muslim in their authentic collections of hadiths: "Whenever we were travelling with the Prophet and came to a tree with extended shade, we left it to God's Messenger (peace be upon him). When we were on the expedition known as Dhat-al-Riqāʿ, the Prophet reclined under a tree after having hung his sword from one of its branches. A man from the idolaters came up to him and drew his sword and said to the Prophet, 'Do you fear me?' The Prophet said, 'No.' The man asked him, 'Who will protect you from me.' The Prophet answered, 'God will protect me from you. Put down that sword.' The man put it down." It is sufficient to remember that this took place during an expedition in which the Muslim army went through great difficulty and when the form of prayer that applies in situations of extreme fear was allowed for the first time.

Another great event that gives credence to this true promise is the Prophet's remarkable attitude in the Battle of Ḥunayn. At one point in the Battle, the Prophet found himself alone, surrounded by the enemy, while the Muslim soldiers were in a panic, running away in all directions. He was riding a mule, and he pushed it to run towards the enemy. His uncle, al-ʿAbbās ibn ʿAbd al-Muṭṭablib, took up its reign trying to restrain it. The unbelievers were soon coming up to him. When they surrounded him, he did not even try to turn back. In fact, he dismounted to make himself an easier target. He said to them: "I am God's Prophet, no doubt. I am ʿAbd al-Muṭṭalib's grandson." In fact, he was challenging them, pointing out his position to them. By God, they could not touch him. For God supported him with His own soldiers and restrained his enemies' hands with His own. This hadith is highly authentic, related by al-Bukhari, Muslim, Ahmad and many others.

Thus God ensured that he stayed among his community, working hard to convey His message and fulfil His trust. When he had completed his task, He revealed to him the verse that says: *"This day I have perfected your religion for you and completed My favours to you. I have chosen self-surrender [i.e. Islam] to be your faith."* (5: 3.)

The examples that we have given so far are prophesies of the first type. They speak of the future of the religion of Islam, and what may happen to the Qur'an or the Prophet. They provide clear proof that the source of the Qur'an is God Himself.

Promises for the Future

The second type of prophesies relate to the future of the new faith and those who accepted its message in the early days. When the Prophet was still in Makkah, with his small band of followers, the Qur'an related to the believers some of the accounts of earlier messengers with the aim of giving

The Qur'an An Eternal Challenge

them reassurance about the future. It promised them victory and security as given to earlier communities of believers: *"Long ago has Our word gone forth to Our servants, the message-bearers, that they indeed are the ones to receive support, and that Our hosts indeed are the ones to achieve victory."* (37: 171-173.) *"We shall indeed give support to Our messengers and those who believe, both in this world's life and on the Day when all the witnesses shall stand up."* (40: 51.)

When the Muslims migrated to Madinah, seeking secure refuge, they thought that they would be able to enjoy a life of peace. Soon, however, they were facing all out war, time after time. This meant that they had actually moved into an even worse state of fear. Their dearest hopes were for a day when they would be able to lay down their arms and feel secure. In those very difficult days the Qur'an was telling them about a future when they would enjoy power and have a kingdom of their own, in addition to what they hoped for of peace and security. Was this merely an exercise to pacify them and calm their worries, or one of dreams and wishful thinking? No, it was a sure promise, given in the most affirmative style and reiterated with an oath: *"God has promised those of you who believe and do righteous deeds that, of a certainty, He will cause them to accede to power on earth, even as He caused [some of] those who lived before them to accede to it; and that, of a certainty, He will firmly establish for them the religion which He has been pleased to bestow on them; and that, of a certainty, He will cause their erstwhile state of fear to be replaced by a sense of security."* (24: 51.)

Al-Ḥākim relates the following report, grading it as authentic, on the authority of Ubay ibn Ka'b, a companion of the Prophet: "When God's Messenger migrated to Madinah with his companions and the Anṣār gave them refuge, all Arabs mounted a campaign of hostility against them. They had to have their arms next to them whenever they went to sleep and when they woke up. Some of them wondered whether they would live to see a day when they would be able to spend their nights in security, fearing none but God. This verse was revealed in answer to that." Ibn Abi Ḥātim reports that "this verse was revealed at a time when we, Muslims, were in great fear."

Reflect, if you will, on how this promise came true in the broadest and

67

The Prophecies of the Qur'an

fullest sense, during the lifetimes of the Prophet's companions themselves. It was a promise made directly to them, as indicated by the phrase, "*God has promised those of you...*" Hence, it was their fear that was replaced by a sense of total security, and they were able to gain power in large areas stretching far to the east and far to the west.

We also need to consider the usage in the last quoted verse of the quality of doing well: "*God has promised those of you who believe and do righteous deeds ...*" The emphasis here is on doing '*righteous deeds*'. We should relate this to another verse that specifies this condition in more detail: "*God will most certainly support those who support His cause. Indeed, God is Most-Powerful, Almighty; [those are] the ones who, [even] if We firmly establish them on earth, attend regularly to their prayer, and give in charity, and enjoin the doing of what is right and forbid the doing of what is wrong.*" (22: 40-41.) This verse tells us much about the reasons for the setbacks the believers sometimes suffered, such as loss of land or military defeat. It is all due to their falling short of meeting the requirements of their faith: "*Why, when a calamity befell you, after you had inflicted twice as much [on your enemy], did you exclaim, 'How has this come about?' Say: 'It has come from your own selves.*" (3: 165.) "*God would never change the blessings with which He has graced a people unless they change their inner selves.*" (8: 53.)

A second example of prophesies relating to the future of Islam and the Muslims may be taken from the events that led to the peace Treaty of Al-Hudaybiyah, concluded between the Prophet and the Quraysh. The terms dictated by the Quraysh specified that the Muslims would not enter Makkah that year. They were allowed to go there the following year, but without any arms other than their swords in their sheaths. In their past experience, the Quraysh were not the people to honour their pledges or observe the values imposed by blood or tribal relations, or even religious values. In fact, at the very point of signing that Treaty, the Quraysh were making a determined effort to prevent the Muslims from fulfilling their religious duties at the Ka‘bah, acknowledged by the Quraysh themselves. What would their real attitude be the following year? Should they honour their promise and allow the Muslims in, how could the Muslims feel secure, when they would be on the Quraysh's home ground, without their body armour and other equipment? Could this be a trick to tempt the Muslims so that they easily fell into the trap?

Such possibilities could not be discounted by any means. Such suspicion is further enhanced by the fact that the Quraysh insisted, as a condition, that the Muslims would not wear any but the minimum of armament. Their swords might reassure the Muslims that they would be able to defend themselves against an attack with similar weapons, but against an attack with spears and arrows they would certainly be defenceless. In such a situation, beset with doubt and suspicion, they received a firm promise comprising all three matters: entering Makkah, security and completing their rituals: *"Indeed, God has shown the truth in His Messenger's true vision: most certainly shall you enter the Inviolable House of Worship, if God so wills, in full security, with your heads shaved or your hair cut short, without any fear."* (48: 27.) That certainly came to pass. They entered Makkah for their compensatory *umrah*, stayed there for three days and completed their rituals.

A third example may be seen in the arguments the unbelievers used against the Muslims when they were still in Makkah, before they migrated to Madinah. The unbelievers argued that the Byzantines also claimed to have revelations from on high, but their revelations and scriptures were of no avail to them in their war against the Majian Persians. You, Muslims, claim that you will overcome us with this Book that you claim to be revealed from on high. But you will see how we will inflict on you a defeat similar to that inflicted by the Majians on the Byzantines. In response, God revealed the opening of Surah 30, The Byzantines: *"Defeated have been the Byzantines in the lands close-by. Yet it is they who, notwithstanding this their defeat, shall be victorious within a few years."* (30: 2-4.)

This report of an impending victory, coming at a particular time, gave two pieces of information regarding future events, each of which was beyond anyone's imagination. The Byzantine Empire had sunk into a sorry state of weakness that culminated in its homeland being attacked and defeated. This is the point the Qur'anic verse refers to as it specifies the location of the defeat, *'in the lands close-by.'* No one gave the Byzantines a remote chance of

3. The Prophecies of the Qur'an

recovery, let alone specified the time when it would attain a military victory. Hence, the unbelievers discounted that promise and bet that it would never be. But the Qur'an did not stop at this. It made a further promise, stating that *"on that day will the believers [too, have cause to] rejoice in victory granted by God."* (30: 4-5.) This statement signified that on the day the Byzantines achieved victory over the Persians, the Muslims would be victorious against the unbelievers. Each one of these two victories was highly improbable by all human standards. What would people say to a promise stating that both would take place on the same day? Hence, the Qur'an makes this prophesy in a most emphatic statement: *"This is God's promise. Never does God fail to fulfil His promise, but most people do not know."* (30: 6.)

God certainly fulfilled His promise, and the Byzantines were able to achieve victory against the Persians in less than nine years, according to all historians. That victory took place on the same day as the victory achieved by a small army of believers against a much larger force of unbelievers, in what came to be known as the Battle of Badr.

It should be pointed out here that the Qur'anic text specifies that the victory of the Byzantines would be *'within a few years'*. The equivalent Arabic expression signifies any number of years between three and nine. Some people may wonder why the Qur'an used this rather indeterminate period, when God is certainly aware of the year, day and exact hour of the event in question. The answer may be found in the fact that people differ in their method of reckoning. Some date according to the lunar calendar, while others use a solar one; some drop any fraction, while others round it up to the next whole number. Hence, it is wiser to give an expression that gives a perfectly true prediction, whatever method of reckoning people employ. This puts an end to all doubt and argument. Besides, there may be a gap of time between the early signs of victory and the time when it ultimately takes place, which may lead to some difference as to the exact timing of victory. All this makes it more appropriate to say, as the Qur'an says, *'within a few years'*, not 'after a few years'.

Future Events Involving the Unbelievers

The third type of prophesies we find in the Qur'an relate to what the future holds for the unbelievers. The first example we will give relates to the hardened attitude the people of Makkah adopted towards the new message of Islam. The Prophet prayed that they would experience years of draught similar to those experienced by the people of Egypt at the time of Joseph. Let us look here at what the Qur'an says in response to that prayer: *"Wait, then, for the Day when the skies shall bring forth a pall of smoke which makes obvious [impending events], enveloping the people: 'Grievous indeed is this suffering.'"* (44: 10-11.)

What did actually take place? They had things very hard, so much so that they had bones for food. A person would look at the sky and see something like smoke covering it. This is mentioned in an authentic hadith related by Al-Bukhari on the authority of ʿAbdullāh ibn Masʿūd. The verses that follow in the surah make this statement: *"Our Lord, relieve us of suffering, for truly we now believe... We will lift this suffering for a little while, although you are bound to revert [to your old ways]; but on the Day when We shall make the most mighty strike, We shall inflict Our retribution."* (44: 12 & 15-16.) When we look carefully at the last two verses, we find in them three predictions: a lifting of the hardship, a return to their evil ways and scheming, and a subsequent retribution inflicted on them. All this actually took place, as is explained in the hadith to which we have just referred.

When the people of Makkah suffered the drought, they came to the Prophet requesting him to pray for rain. They also made an earnest prayer, appealing to God to remove their suffering and asserting that they were now believers: *"Our Lord, relieve us of suffering, for truly we now believe."* (44: 12.) God sent them rain, and their land bloomed again. But it did not take them long to revert to their old, evil ways, behaving arrogantly and denying the truth. Thus God caused them to suffer a most mighty strike at Badr, when

The Prophecies of the Qur'an

no less than 70 of their brave warriors were killed and a similar number were taken captive by the Muslims.

Makkan Qur'anic revelations speak about God's retribution in various ways. Sometimes the reference is made in general, unspecified terms, like: "*As for the unbelievers - in result of their [evil] deeds, sudden calamities will always befall them or will alight close to their homes, until God's promise is fulfilled.*" (13: 31.) "*Hence, turn you aside for a while from those [unbelievers], and see them. In time, they will surely come to see.*" (37: 174-175.)

At other times, the suffering is specified to take the form of a military defeat. The clearest example is the verse that states: "*The hosts shall be routed, and they shall turn their backs in flight.*" (54: 45.) A similar reference is included in one of the earliest surahs of the Qur'an to be revealed: "*He knows that in time there will be among you sick people, and others who will go about the land in search of God's bounty, and others who will fight in God's cause.*" (73: 20.) Such reports of future events, made as they were in the early days of Islam, when the Prophet and his companions were still in Makkah are most remarkable. At the time, no one could have contemplated any prospect of war and meeting of armies and hosts, let alone their flight and defeat. Indeed, when the first of these verses was revealed, ʿUmar wondered: 'To which host does this verse refer?' He later reported: 'On the day of the Battle of Badr, I saw God's Messenger reading it.'

On other occasions, the reference is more remarkable, as it specifies particular details. A case in mind is that of the man who used to denounce the Qur'an and describe it as 'fables of the ancient people'. The Qur'an says about this man, who many reports name as al-Walīd ibn al-Mughīrah of the Makhzūm branch of Quraysh: "*We shall brand him on the snout.*" (68: 16.) As the verse is worded, it may also be rendered as: "We shall brand him with indelible disgrace." The man was hit by a sword on the nose during the Battle of Badr, and that produced a mark which became the subject of people's ridicule for the rest of his life. Thus, what is prophesied in the verse took place putting into effect both meanings of the Qur'anic statement.

While these predictions concerned the unbelievers of the Arabian tribe of the Quraysh, similar predictions are made with regard to the Jews. Here are some: *"They cannot harm you beyond causing you some trifling hurt; and if they fight against you they will turn their backs upon you in flight. Then they will receive no help. Ignominy shall be pitched over them wherever they may be, save when they have a bond with God and a bond with men."* (3: 111-112.) *"Your Lord made it known that most certainly He would rouse against them, until Resurrection Day, people who would afflict them with cruel suffering."* (7: 167.)

One wonders at these verses. Are they made up of letters and words? Or are they chains and handcuffs from which they can have no release? Do you not see that ever since this judgement was slammed over their heads, they remained scattered all over the world, subjugated by other communities, without a state of their own upholding their cause? Although they have amassed great financial wealth, to the extent that they control nearly half the world's wealth, they remain in their Diaspora, unable to form for themselves even a small state.² In the Christian countries of the West, they are often subjected to different types of persecution and ultimate rejection. In Muslim countries, traditionally the most hospitable of places, they are accepted only as a community subject to the law of the land, not as a ruling community.

Have you heard what they have been scheming of late? Their dreams have concentrated on making the Holy Land a place for their national home, where they hope to converge from different places of the world. Then, when they will have lived there for sometime without being driven out, they will try to remove their historical stigma by re-establishing their old kingdom in that land. Indeed, in pursuit of this dream, they have been emigrating to Palestine individually and in small groups to make of Palestine their place of settlement. One wonders, have they been able to take this initial step – or should we say this first and last step – relying on their own strength? Definitely not. They could only achieve it through having a bond with other people, exactly as the

---

2- The author wrote this part of the book during the 1930s, long before the state of Israel came into being with the help of the US, Europe and the UN.

The Prophecies of the Qur'an

above-quoted Qur'anic verse says. God certainly tells the truth.

They may dream that when they compete with the indigenous people of Palestine for their land, they pave the way for taking full control over it. But this is a dream which will certainly be dashed against the great barriers that stand in the way of its fulfilment. They want to change God's words, but His words cannot be changed by anyone. *"Have they, perchance, a share in (God's) dominion? If so, they would not give other people so much as [would fill] the groove of a date-stone."* (4: 53.) They may design and scheme, but God will foil their evil scheming, if He so wills.

We have so far looked at examples of Qur'anic prophesies that penetrate through the thick curtains screening the near and distant future. They even control the nature of events and their timing. Indeed as time passes, it brings only what confirms them in totality and detail, and whether they speak of something close or very far away.

When we look at all that the Qur'an includes of news, we find that Muhammad (peace be upon him) tackles something that lies beyond his own feelings and intellectual faculties, whether they relate to the past, present or future. Indeed, when he speaks about the past, every evidence of history confirms what he says, and when he talks about the future, everything he says will inevitably come to pass. Furthermore, if he speaks about God, the angels and the realm that lies beyond the reach of human perception, we find confirmation of what he says in earlier Scriptures and the statements of earlier prophets.

At this juncture, a question is raised: could this man, unlettered and uneducated as he was, have coined up all this discourse himself? The ready, immediate and unhesitating answer is that he must have derived such information from an accurate scientific source, and relied on broad and careful study. Such information could never have come out of his own intelligence and ingenuity. Never had any person, intelligent and resourceful as he might be, been given a guarantee of immunity from error in revealing past historical events or future ones, ancient as the former might have been, or distant as the latter may be.

The prophets themselves, who were among the most intelligent people in history as all their contemporaries have testified, did not receive such a guarantee, even concerning events that were close to them in time and place. Apart from conveying God's revelations, when prophets exercised their own discretion concerning what might have taken place away from them, their judgement might be right or wrong. Jacob, for example, twice accused his sons of fabrication: when they produced Joseph's shirt with blood stains on it and when they told him that his other son had stolen something. Each time he said to them: *"No, but your minds have tempted you to evil. Sweet patience!"* (12: 18 & 83.) He was right concerning the first incident, but wrong with regard to the second. They were innocent of the fabrication he accused them of having perpetrated. Moses (peace be upon him) said to the sage he met: *"You will find me patient, if God so wills, and I shall not disobey you in anything."* (18: 69.) He soon forgot his pledge and showed little patience. Indeed, he did not obey his orders at all.

Muhammad himself (peace be upon him) was subject to people's attempts to give him false evidence so that he would issue an unjust verdict or defend a guilty person, thinking that he was innocent. He only corrected himself when God, who knows all, gave him the right information.

If anyone doubts this, let him read the following verses:

> *We have bestowed this Book on you from on high, setting forth the truth, so that you may judge between people in accordance with what God has taught you. Hence, do not contend with those who betray their trust. Seek God's forgiveness, for God is indeed much-forgiving, merciful. And do not argue on behalf of those who are false to their own selves. Indeed God does not love those who betray their trust and persist in sinful action. They conceal their doings from men, but they cannot conceal them from God; for He is present with them when, in the darkness of the night, they agree all manner of sayings which displease Him. God certainly encompasses [with His knowledge] whatever they*

3 The Prophecies of the Qur'an

do. You may well argue on their behalf in the life of this world, but who is there to argue on their behalf with God on the Day of Resurrection, or who will be their advocate? He who does evil or wrongs his own soul, and then prays to God to forgive him, shall find God much-forgiving, merciful. For he who commits a sin, does so to his own hurt. God is indeed all-knowing, wise. But he who commits a fault or a sin and then throws the blame therefore on an innocent person, burdens himself with both falsehood and a flagrant sin. But for God's grace to you and His mercy, some of them would indeed endeavour to lead you astray. Yet none but themselves do they lead astray. Nor can they harm you in any way. It is God who has bestowed this Book on you from on high and given you wisdom, and has taught you what you did not know. God's favour on you is great indeed. (4: 105-113.)

An authentic report on the reason for the revelation of these verses says that a thief entered the place of an Anṣāri man called Rifāʿah, forcing his entry and stealing all the food and weapons that were there. In the morning, the Anṣāri looked for his belongings until he was certain that they were in a house belonging to the Ubayriq clan, some of whom were hypocrites. He sent his nephew to complain to the Prophet, who told him: "I will look into the matter." When that clan heard this, they came to the Prophet and said: "Messenger of God, Qatādah ibn al-Nuʿmān and his uncle Rifāʿah have been accusing a certain family of our clan of theft, without evidence or proof, although that family are good Muslims." Qatādah later came to the Prophet who told him: "You have been speaking about a Muslim family, who have been mentioned to me as people of piety, and accusing them of theft without evidence or proof." Qatādah went back to his uncle and told him what the Prophet had said. His uncle simply said: "I appeal to God for help." Shortly after that, the verses quoted above were revealed, making it clear that the Ubayriq clan were making false statements and commanding the Prophet to seek forgiveness for what he had said to Qatādah.[3] [This hadith is related by

---

3- The incident and the full significance of these verses are discussed in detail in Sayyal-Tirmidhi and al-Ḥākim, with the latter classifying it as highly authentic.]

Now look at what the Prophet says about himself in a hadith related by Ahmad and Ibn Mājah: "I am only a man like you whose opinions may be right or wrong. But when I tell you, 'God says', then know that I will never tell a lie against God." He also says: "I am only a human being and you bring your disputes to me. It may be that some of you may have a stronger argument or a better evidence than others, and I would then think that he is telling the truth and rule in his favour. If I give any of you something that belongs by right to another Muslim, I am only giving him a brand of fire. He may then take it or leave it." [Related by Mālik, al-Bukhari, Muslim and others.] A person who is so unable to know the truth of what might have taken place between two people whom he has seen and heard in his own time and place is undoubtedly less able to know what took place in past history or what will take place in the future.

All that belongs to a different realm, the realm that lies beyond the reach of human perception. As we approach the boundaries of that realm, insight and intelligence have no role. The human mind becomes powerless. It might hit upon the truth once in every several cases where it would otherwise be wrong. Moreover, when it happens to point to something right, there is no guarantee that it will remain free of any change. Indeed, it may disappear by coincidence as it was hit upon by coincidence: *"Had it [i.e. the Qur'an] issued from anyone but God, they would surely have found in it many an inner contradiction."* (4: 82.)

---

id Qutb's *In the Shade of the Qur'an*, The Islamic Foundation, Leicestershire, 2001, Volume 3, pp. 295-306.

Chapter 4

Muhammad's Teacher

It is inevitable that anyone who seeks to learn the source of the Qur'an should expand the area of his investigation. If he cannot establish that source when he considers the insight and intelligence of the person who delivered the Qur'an, he should surely look for it, and find it, inevitably, in education and study. A speaker either composes what he says or copies it from another source. There is no other alternative.

The man reciting and conveying the Qur'an to people was not someone who could himself refer to books and encyclopaedias. Even his enemies admit that he grew up and lived without receiving any education. He was indeed unlettered. At no time did he learn to read a book or to write anything with his own hand. He must, then, have had a teacher who taught him all this information, not by writing but by reading the same to him. This is the logical conclusion at least.

We may well wonder who this teacher was. This is indeed the second point in our question about the Qur'an. Now if we reflect on the proofs and evidences we have regarding the first point of this question, we will find with it information relevant to this second point. We will, in short, be able to determine who this teacher was. In the following pages, we will try to bring this teacher into the limelight, so that the reader will agree with us when we say about him: "This teacher is no human being! This is indeed a noble angel, delivering a message from God, the Lord of all worlds."

Muhammad's Teacher

That Muhammad (peace be upon him) could not have had a teacher from among his illiterate people, who had natural literary gifts but no education, is something everyone readily accepts. Perhaps no one needs to seek any further evidence beyond the fact that Muhammad's people were generally called, 'the illiterate', an appellation indicating that they had no knowledge of religion and faith. The period that preceded the advent of Islam in Arabia is described as *jāhiliyyah*, meaning the period or state of ignorance. Such people, lacking even the very basis of knowledge such that their description was coined from the word 'ignorance', can never stand in a position to teach others, let alone teach their own teacher, he who frequently describes them as ignorant and who relates some aspects of their ignorance in several surahs of his book. Some people suggest that if we want to know the extent of the Arab's ignorance, we only have to read what comes after verse 100 of Surah 6, 'Cattle'".

As for the fact that he had no teacher from among any other community we say that it is sufficient for us to refer anyone who seeks such information to any history source, old or new, Islamic or international. After he has exhausted all possible sources we will ask him whether he has read a single line saying that Muhammad ibn ᶜAbdullāh had met, before declaring himself as Prophet, any scholar and learnt from him any religious knowledge, or heard from him accounts of past nations and communities.

We do not have to give any evidence other than throwing out this challenge in order to prove that nothing of this ever took place. The burden of proof is fairly and squarely on anyone who makes a different claim. Let anyone show us his proof if what he claims be true. We certainly do not say that he never met or saw any such scholar either before or after he became a Prophet. We know that in his childhood, he met a monk called Baḥīra in Busra in southern Syria. In Makkah also, he met a scholar named Waraqah ibn Nawfal shortly after he began to receive revelations from on high, which was about 30 months before he announced his prophethood. We also know that after he started to receive his message, he met numerous Jewish rabbis and Christian priests in Madinah. But the claim we are making is very specific: Muhammad did not learn anything from any such scholar, neither before nor after he was chosen as a prophet. Indeed, before prophethood he never heard anything from them whatsoever relating to religion.

As for those he met after prophethood he spoke and listened to them, but they were the ones who asked and he was the one who answered. He indeed taught, admonished and warned them, and also gave some of them happy news. In the case of those whom he met before or shortly after his prophethood, he had a witness with him on each occasion. His uncle, Abu Ṭālib, was his companion when he met the monk from Syria, while his wife, Khadījah, was in his company when he met Waraqah. So what did his two companions hear of the teachings of these two? Should we not find in history an account of what took place at these two meetings? How come history remains silent on such a remarkable encounter in which all the knowledge of the Qur'an and its accounts of events taking place from the beginning to the end of the world were summed up in a short interview?

Besides, why did his opponents, keen as they were to refute his argument, not take such an encounter as clear proof against him. After all, they did not hesitate to drum up even the slightest hint of suspicion in order to brand him a liar. This was easy proof. Indeed, had it been true, it would have been much more forceful in disproving his claims than all the stubborn opposition they put up. The fact that history has remained silent on this point is sufficient proof that it did not happen. This is not something simple to be overlooked, even by those who were keen to find anything they could to use against the Prophet and his message.

History though has not remained silent. It tells us exactly what happened with these two people. It relates that the Syrian monk saw in the young boy he met sufficient evidence of his future prophethood, as described in earlier Scriptures. This prompted him to tell his uncle: "This boy shall have a great future." History also tells us that when Waraqah ibn Nawfal listened to the Prophet giving him a detailed account of how revelations were given to him, he identified the characteristics of the angel who brought revelations

Muhammad's Teacher

to Moses. He acknowledged him as a prophet and expressed his wish to live longer so that he could be among his supporters.

Whoever respects history and believes in the events as they took place will find that these provide an argument in our favour. But the one who is so shameless as to add to history something he invents may say that Muhammad was a learner in these encounters. Let such a person say what he wants. What his fabrication will produce is, inevitably, a self-contradictory account. What logic would support a claim that a man who saw in someone signs of prophethood long before it became a reality and gave him such news, or one who believed in him after he began to receive his message, would assume the position of teacher of such a Prophet! Do people who make such a claim not reflect on the import of their false allegations?

We ask again: was there at the time any scholar who could impart his knowledge to Muhammad and leave the stamp of that knowledge on the Qur'an?

Even atheists say: "The Qur'an is a single historical work that most accurately reflects the spirit of its age." This is indeed true in as far as its literal meaning goes. The Qur'an reflects that spirit, but is not influenced by it, or we may say that the Qur'an reflects that spirit before it destroys it completely.

We accept their admission and call on them to contemplate the clear picture the Qur'an draws as an example of contemporary scholars. We ask them to read Surahs 2 and 3, respectively entitled The Cow and The House of Imran, and reflect on the arguments these Surahs put to Jewish and Christian scholars concerning faith, history and religious laws and rules. Or let them read any surah that contains a reference to the people of earlier Scriptures, whether they are of the Makkah or Madinah revelations, and consider how the Qur'an describes them. Indeed, the Qur'an describes their knowledge as sheer ignorance, their beliefs as errors and superstition, and their deeds as abominable crimes.

Should we need more and clearer information, here are some examples of how the Qur'an refutes their historical errors. *"O people of earlier revelations! Why do you argue about Abraham, seeing that the Torah and the Gospel were not revealed till long after him? Will you not use your reason?"* (3: 65.) *"Do you claim that Abraham, Ishmael, Isaac, Jacob and their descendants were Jews or Christian?"* (2: 140.) *"The first House of worship ever set up for mankind was indeed the one at Makkah."* (3: 96.) This refutes their claim that their place of worship, which they face in their prayer, predated the Kaʿbah. *"All food was lawful for the children of Israel, except what Israel had made unlawful to himself before the Torah was revealed from on high."* (3: 93.) This verse refutes their claim that camel meat was forbidden to Abraham.

Refuting Absurdity

Let us now look at how the Qur'an refutes their religious superstitions. *"We have created the heavens and the earth and all that is between them in six aeons, and no weariness has ever touched Us."* (50: 38.) This refutes their claim that after God had created all creation in six days, He rested on the seventh day. *"It was not Solomon that denied the truth."* (2: 102.) This vindicates Solomon against their false claim that he was not a prophet, but merely a magician who was able to ride the wind. *"God has heard those who said, 'God is poor and we are rich.'"* (3: 181.) *"The Jews say: 'God's hands are fettered.'"* (5: 64.) *"The Jews said, 'Ezra is son of God,' while the Christians said, 'Jesus is son of God.'"* (9: 30.) *"The Jews and the Christians say, We are God's children, and His beloved ones." "Disbelievers are they who say, God is the Christ, son of Mary". "Disbelievers are they who say, God is the third of a trinity."* (5: 18, 72 & 73.) *"Say: People of earlier revelations! Come to an equitable agreement between you and us: that we shall worship none but God, and that we shall associate no partners with Him, and that we shall not take one another for lords beside God."* (3: 64.)

Muhammad's Teacher

Consider now how the Qur'an describes the faith of religious leaders at the time of its revelation, particularly those who were Christian. Elements of polytheism were so evident in their religion. Indeed, the illiterate Arabs noticed this and consoled themselves on account of their own polytheism: *"When the son of Mary is set forth as an example, your own people raise an outcry on this score, and say, 'Which is better - our deities or he?'"* (43: 57.) They even used Jesus in their argument that the monotheism which the Qur'an advocates was an innovation without precedent in all religions. They said: *"Never did we hear of a claim like this in any faith of latter days."* (38: 7.) In this they are referring particularly to Christianity.

Here is yet another series of offences which the Qur'an relates as their long chain of crimes:

> *And so, [We punished them] for the breaking of their pledge, their disbelief in God's revelations, their killing of prophets against all right, and for their boast, "Our hearts are closed". Indeed God sealed their hearts on account of their disbelief. As a result they have no faith except for a few of them. And for their disbelief and the monstrous calumny they utter against Mary, and their boast: "We have killed the Christ Jesus, son of Mary, God's Messenger." They did not kill him, and neither did they crucify him, but it only seemed to them [as if it had been] so. Those who hold conflicting views about him are indeed confused, having no real knowledge about it, and following mere conjecture. For, of a certainty, they did not kill him. No! God raised him up to Himself. God is indeed Almighty, Wise. There is not one of the people of earlier revelations but will, at the moment of his death, believe in him, and on the Day of Resurrection he will bear witness to the truth against them. So, then, for the wrongdoing of the Jews did We forbid them some of the good things of life which had been formerly allowed to them; and, indeed for their turning away often from God's path, and for their taking usury although it had been forbidden to them, and their wrongful devouring of other people's property. We have prepared for the unbelievers among them grievous suffering.* (4: 155-161.)

Do we see in all this a picture of teachers imparting their knowledge to the one who conveyed the Qur'an to mankind? Certainly not, for it is the reverse which is true. He is the one who teaches them and points out their errors and their poor knowledge.

We do not deny that there were among them some scholars of rich knowledge. But those of them who were deeply rooted in knowledge declared their belief in the Qur'an and the Prophet who delivered it: *"None can bear witness between me and you as God does; and anyone who possesses knowledge of the revelations."* (13: 43.) Had they been his teachers, they would have believed in themselves, instead of believing in him.

We should also raise the question: was the knowledge possessed by scholars available to anyone who sought it? On the contrary, they were so secretive about their knowledge, that they guarded it more preciously than they did their own lives. They were reluctant to impart it even to their own children, fearing for their positions or hoping themselves to be chosen as the prophet whom they knew would soon be coming.

Let us refer to the Qur'an which the atheists have accepted as an arbiter between them and us. It provides the complete answer to this question. It tells us that in their keen desire to keep their Scriptures and knowledge to themselves they would *"write out the Scriptures with their own hands and then say, 'This is from God,' in order to exchange it for a trifling price."* (2: 79.) At times they would *"twist their tongues when quoting the Scriptures, so that you may think that [what they say] is from the Scriptures, when it is not from the Scriptures. They say: It is from God, when it is not from God."* (3: 78.) At other times they would *"distort the meaning of [God's] words."* (5: 13.) They would also resort to dividing their Scriptures, revealing some parts and keeping others secret: *"Say: Who has bestowed from on high the Scriptures which Moses brought to men as a light and a guidance, and which you treat as mere sheets of paper, making a show of them the while you conceal much."* (6: 91.) Sometimes they argued citing what they had learnt by heart. They looked dumbfounded when they were told to bring the Torah and read it to prove any point they could. They would not take that up. Alternatively, they might bring it and read the verses preceding and following the relevant one, concealing that verse with their own hands. This actually took place when they denied that the Torah specified stoning as a punishment for adultery. [This story is related by al-Bukhari in his *Ṣaḥīḥ*.]

The Qur'an openly accuses them of deceit and of concealing the truth: *"O people of earlier revelations! Why do you cloak the truth with falsehood and conceal the truth of which you are so well aware?"* (3: 71.) Indeed, the Qur'an brings into the open that which they had concealed and arbitrates on that over which they disputed. *"O people of the Bible! Now Our Messenger has come to you to make clear to you much of what you have been concealing of the Bible."* (5: 15.) *"The Qur'an explains to the Children of Israel most of that over which they hold divergent views."* (27: 76.) *"By God, even before your time We sent messengers to various communities; but Satan has made all their own doings seem goodly to them; and he is their patron today. Hence, grievous suffering awaits them. And upon you have We bestowed from on high this Book so that you may make clear to them all questions on which they hold divergent views, and provide guidance and bestow grace on people who will believe."* (16: 63-64.)

It is important to reflect on these last two quotations, from Surahs 27 & 16, entitled respectively The Ant and The Bee. Both were revealed in Makkah, i.e. in the early period of Islam. Yet both make it clear that an essential purpose of the revelation of the Qur'an is to explain to the people of earlier Scriptures questions on which they dispute. This is actually the first purpose, followed by providing guidance to the believers and bestowing mercy on them.

Once more we say to anyone who claims that a human being taught Muhammad what he preached: tell us the name of that teacher, and who saw and heard him, and what he heard him saying? When and where did this teaching take place? To us, the term, 'human', refers to people who walk on the earth, and whom we see as they come and go. Hence, we do not accept such a claim without naming the man in question. Otherwise, the claim is the same as that made by people who allege that God has partners who do not exist anywhere other than in their imagination. They too are required to name those partners: *"Yet they ascribe to God partners. Say: Name them. Would you tell Him of anything on earth which He does not know; or are these merely empty words?"* (13: 33.)

And we ask: was this prophet born on Mars, or was he brought up in a remote corner of the world, and then came to his people after he had attained maturity? Did they see him only sparingly thereafter? Was he not in fact born in their midst? Was he not among them all the time, meeting them morning and evening? Did they not see him coming and going? *"Or is it that they have not recognised their Messenger, and so they disavow him?"* (23: 69.)

Yes, indeed. In their hostility to his cause, his people contrived to make such a claim: *"It is but a human being that teaches him!"* (16: 103.) But were they serious about their claim? Were they referring to a person whom they knew to have such great knowledge? No. They were not even concerned about being right or serious. They only wanted to defend themselves against their inability to make a serious reply to his call. Hence, they selected whatever defence came to their minds, be it true or false, serious or trifling.

Then, who was this human being they said was teaching him? Did they dare to attribute this teaching to one of their own number? No. They realised their ignorance was so manifest that they could not teach a man who spoke to them about things that neither they nor their ancestors knew anything about.

Should we suggest that, having found Makkah devoid of scholars of religion and history at the time when Muhammad was sent with his message, they attributed that teaching to a scholar in Madinah or Syria or some other place? They were unable to make such a claim either. Then who could that teacher be?

4 Muhammad's Teacher

The Honour Conferred

They realised that they had to seek a person who met two conditions. The first that he lived in Makkah, so that it would be plausible for them to allege that he met him morning and evening to impart his instruction. The second that he belonged to a different race and faith. This would make it easier for them to claim that such a person could impart to him knowledge that they themselves lacked. When they looked for a person who met these two conditions they only came up with a Greek blacksmith.

Yes, they were able to produce none other than a young man who was well known in the market place, but not in study circles. Unlike them, he was neither illiterate nor an idolater. He was a Christian who could read and write. Hence, he could be, according to them, a suitable teacher for Muhammad, and a scholar who could teach all Christian monks and Jewish rabbis, as well as the world at large. Let us now enquire about this man: was he given to scholarly pursuits, studying books and able to distinguish the truth from falsehood in what they contained? Was he equipped with the mental faculties of perception and understanding that would make him suitable for this role? Our investigation shows that he was an ordinary blacksmith using his tools for his living. His mental power was that of an ordinary uneducated labourer, whose knowledge of books and learning did not exceed wishful thinking. Besides, he read in a foreign language that was unknown to Muhammad and his people. But none of this was sufficient to deprive him of the title of Muhammad's teacher and mentor.

Thus, the serious circle was too narrow for them. They could only function in the open fields of absurdity. Indeed they took this so far that even they themselves could not be taken seriously by anyone. They were just like one who said that knowledge could come out of ignorance, and that man may receive the faculty of speech from a parrot! We need say no more. *"We certainly know that they say, 'It is but a human being that teaches him!' [notwithstanding that] the tongue of him to whom they so maliciously point is wholly outlandish, whereas this is Arabic speech, clear in itself and clearly showing the truth."* (16: 103.)

They simply found the whole idea so funny that they approved the falsehood it implied. The whole picture looked to them full of mockery, and they laughed loudly at it as they felt it gave them their revenge. Little did they realise that they were mocking themselves. In fact it was an admission by them that they were the most ignorant community on earth. They actually acknowledged that any foreigner, even an uneducated blacksmith, had greater knowledge than what their whole community enjoyed. They would have been much better off remaining silent than to make such a claim. Inevitably, it all backfired on them.

The truth, with which they were at loggerheads, has gained in power as a result of their false allegations. When they tried to find a human being whom they alleged imparted knowledge to Muhammad, they could not claim that that source was a foreigner. They wanted him to come from within Muhammad's home town. When they could find none, their last resort was to produce the blacksmith. The point arises: if that young blacksmith had such a great treasure of knowledge, what prevented them from learning from him like Muhammad did, according to their false claims? This would easily have solved their problem, for then they would have had the same knowledge as Muhammad. Indeed if that young man was the sort of teacher they claimed, what prevented him from opening his knowledge out to the rest of the world, so that he could be acknowledged as a teacher or leader of mankind?

Besides, why did they not attribute those disciplines unknown to them to the people who spent a lifetime learning them, such as the Jewish rabbis in Madinah or the Christian priests in Syria? This would certainly have been more plausible and more convincing. This claim could have been promoted much more easily than the one attributing such knowledge to a blacksmith in Makkah. Was the whole earth too narrow for them that they could not find a more knowledgeable person in religion and history than that blacksmith? The fact is that they considered a claim of foreign teaching even less plausible and certainly unacceptable. Had they resorted to it, they would have been more forcefully accused of arrogant obstinacy. Hence they felt

Muhammad's Teacher

that they needed to narrow the circle of their accusations. But their falsehood has been easily seen for what it is.

These were Muhammad's people, his most hardened opponents. They were fully aware of his travels, movements and other actions. Yet they were totally unable to establish any learning contact between him and the people of knowledge in his own time. Nevertheless, the atheists of today, more than thirteen centuries after his message, when all events have been determined and all accounts settled, persist in trying to establish such a connection. What is even more singular is that they try to find such a connection in historical garbage, and in an area which his own people could not lower themselves to investigate.

We tell them to spare themselves such efforts. The Quraysh, Muhammad's tribe, had exhausted it long before them. Let them turn away from this area, for logic and history have shown that all such attempts are destined to miserable failure. If they persist, they should know that any doubt that is raised against the clear truth will be turned to the truth's advantage and favour.

A Worthless, False Allegation

Had the allegation that Muhammad received all the knowledge contained in the Qur'an from a human teacher been an expression of an idea or a doubt felt by those who made it, they would have held on to it without moving to something different. If the human mind were to try to explain the total break between Muhammad's life before receiving his message and after it, it will inevitably conclude that the new knowledge Muhammad expressed must have been imparted to him by fresh instruction. Since people do not know of any teachers on earth who are not human, the first thing that comes to mind is that there must be a man who has undertaken this fresh instruction and imparted its content to Muhammad. Had there been even the slightest possibility that a person making such an allegation could find real or plausible factors which would give him even the slightest conviction within himself that this was the case, he would stick to it and would not seek a different explanation. But those who make such allegations continue, even to this day, to be uncertain as to what to say about the Qur'an: should they claim that it was taught to Muhammad by another man, or should they say that it is the product of his own intellect, as mentioned earlier, or should they combine the two claims together, describing the Prophet as being 'taught' and a 'madman', as the Qur'an reports in verse 14 of Surah 44?

The allegation that the Qur'an was taught to Muhammad by a human being was the least frequent argument employed by those who denied that the Qur'an was revealed by God. Instead, their most frequent argument was that it was self inspiration, although they could not agree on what psychological condition experienced by the Prophet led to the production of the Qur'an, and whether it was poetic inspiration, madness or mere dreaming. Remember, all these arguments are reported in the Qur'an itself.

They tried every angle and possibility to come up with something to support their rejection of the message of the Qur'an. They did not stop at the limits that might reasonably be applied to serious speech like the Qur'an, or to a highly serious and wise mind like the Prophet's. They even considered the most extreme psychological conditions that produce human speech, whether the speaker be rational or irrational. This is clear evidence that they were not trying to prove an allegation they truly believed. They simply raised all possibilities and exhausted all options, overlooking all the defects therein. Basically, they were heedless of all improbability. They simply wanted to raise doubts in the minds of those who sought to know the truth and to learn the true faith.

Yet they were never satisfied with any opinion they advanced. Whenever they took up an opinion and tried to apply it to the Qur'an, they found that it was far from suitable. No plausible argument could be used to prove it. Hence, they would quickly move to try a different opinion, then a third one, and every time they realised that all their attempts were futile. They remained

Muhammad's Teacher

in doubt, torn between these views which they knew to be false. If you wish to look at a picture describing their persistent confusion, you need only read the following verse of the Qur'an: *"They say: Nay, [Muhammad propounds] the most involved and confusing of dreams! Nay, but he has invented all this! Nay, but he is only a poet!"* (21: 5.)

Look at how many times the conjunction indicating a switch of direction is used. This on its own depicts their state of confusion and how they were totally unable to agree on any thing. It simply describes how a perjurer switches from one extreme to another when he feels that his lies are about to be discovered. Haphazardly, he seeks anything to help him support his untenable position. *"See to what they liken you, [Prophet], simply because they have gone astray and are now unable to find a way [to the truth]."* (17: 48 & 25: 9.)

This is the same position adopted today by modern atheists who attribute the Qur'an to 'self inspiration'. They allege that their view relies on modern scientific discoveries. But theirs is no new opinion. It is, in substance and detail, the same as the old one advanced by former day opponents in the society of ignorant Arabia. Those people of old described the Prophet as a man with a great and active imagination, as possessing a profound sensitivity, all of which made of him a poet. Then they added that his emotions overpowered his senses to the extent that he could imagine that he was seeing and hearing someone speaking to him, while the reality of what he saw and heard was no more than his own emotions and feelings. Thus, they attributed it all to madness or dreaming. But they could not persevere with such 'explanations'. So they abandoned the notion of 'self inspiration' when they realised that the Qur'an included accounts of past and future communities. They thought that he might have heard these from the scholars he met during his travels. This would mean that a human being had taught it all to him. So what is new in all this? Is it not a new version reflecting the old allegations of the ignorant Quraysh? Indeed neo-atheism is no more than an updated or distorted version of the former type in its oldest of guises.

Modern ideas are fed by the left-overs of past, ignorant days: "*Even thus, the same as they say, spoke those who lived before their time; their hearts are all alike.*" (2: 118.)

Yet they acknowledged, in spite of all what they said about him, that the Prophet Muhammad was exemplary in his honesty. They added that he could be excused in attributing his vision to Divine inspiration, because his dreams were so vivid that he thought it so. Hence, he only said what he believed. In the Qur'an, God tells us that their forerunners took the same attitude: "*It is not that they give you the lie, but the evildoers simply deny God's revelations.*" (6: 33.) If he is justified in describing what he saw and heard as revelation, what justification had he in saying that neither he nor his people ever heard such news, when they alleged that he had heard them before? In fact, to be consistent, they have to claim that it was all fabrication, but they do not wish to make such a claim so as to give themselves a guise of fairness and objectivity. Yet by adopting such an attitude they practically make that accusation, although they may not perceive it as so.

Chapter 5

A Source Beyond Man's World

All that we have said so far confirms the fact that there is no human source from which the Qur'an was derived, neither from within the man who delivered it nor from any human being. Anyone who tries to make it a 'human production' comes unstuck. Confused, overweening and stubborn, his failure is manifest. Hence, we need to move on and look for a source of the Qur'an outside the human domain altogether. We must not stop at the point unbelievers, old and modern, reached, attributing the Qur'an to self inspiration at times, and to human teaching at others, or to a mixture of both. Logic dictates that we should reject what has been proved, by strong evidence, to be false. In fact we should follow the logical argument until we find the clear truth.

The unbelievers claim that they have refrained from following the logical argument only because they respect natural laws and understand the reasons which make people say something or another, whether based on personal logic and experience or reporting what others may have said. Faithful to natural science, as they claim themselves to be, they do not go beyond its domain in order to look for something they do not see or experience. We have seen, however, that this attitude has turned against them. For it causes them to overstep the natural limits of reason and history, leading them to self-contradiction, to changing history, and to forcing things out of their nature. What reasonable person would adopt such an attitude, spurning his own reason in order to follow his habits!

5. A Source Beyond Man's World

The truth is that they have another reason which prevents them from joining us in our pursuit, but they try to conceal it. This is the fact that they feel too proud to acknowledge leadership to a man who, all of a sudden, claims himself to be God's Messenger, having the right to be obeyed in what he orders or forbids. This man also puts the hard facts before their eyes, separating them from their past to which they want to cling, and from their desires which they want to fulfil: "*He has brought them the truth, and the truth do most of them detest!*" (23: 70.) Therefore, we will leave them where they wish to remain. We will continue our pursuit of the truth, praying to God to guide us to it. By His grace we shall have that guidance.

The Way Revelation Is Given

We now move into a third area of our discussion about the source of the Qur'an. The first tried to establish whether the Qur'an could have been the result of some factors from within the Prophet's own self. The second looked at the possibility of it being taught to Muhammad by a human teacher. In this third area we will look at the possibility of the Qur'an having a source higher than the human realm. But we will not be wondering aimlessly here, nor will our pursuit lead us to remote corners or distant places. We will limit our investigation to a certain area where we feel we may find the secret we are looking for. We will simply study the direct situations when the Qur'an was being issued through Muhammad (peace be upon him).

We have all heard of the remarkable phenomenon that was visible in his noble face every time a Qur'anic revelation was sent down to him from on high. It was apparent to everyone who looked at him. They saw his face suddenly turning red, and he would turn hot to the extent that sweat drops gathered on his forehead. He became heavy, to the extent that his thigh would press hard against the thigh of the person next to him. If he was riding, his mount would sit down. At the same time, babbling noises, sounding like the buzzing of bees, were heard near his face. [All these descriptions have been confirmed in authentic hadiths related by al-Bukhari, Muslim and others.] Soon after all this, he relaxed and recited new Qur'anic verses that had not previously been known.

This is the nearest area in which to look for the source of the Qur'an. It is here that investigation should proceed, because here the truth will be determined. When we have a causal relationship between two different matters, so as whenever one takes place the other materialises, then a proper investigation of that relationship will show us the true cause of the effect we have.

Let us now consider that phenomenon: was it deliberately affected, even as a preparatory means to achieve higher concentration? Or was it something entirely involuntary? If the latter, then was it induced by any normal situation, such as lethargy or drowsiness, or an abnormal one such as mental disturbance? Or was it a reaction to something totally external?

A glance at the components of that phenomenon is sufficient to show that it could never have been the result of affectation. This is even more apparent when we reflect on the aspect of babbling noises heard near the Prophet's face. Moreover, if such a condition was affected, it could easily have been resorted to at any time. Whenever he wished to have more of the Qur'an, Muhammad would have been able to produce it by resorting to this method of preparation. Thus, the Qur'an would be available to him at will. However, we know that on the many occasions when he desperately needed it, he could only receive it when God willed that it be revealed. Hence, it was clearly an involuntary process.

If we look at it again we find that it is in no way like the drowsiness we experience when we are in need of sleep. The Prophet experienced this condition in all situations, sitting or standing, walking or riding, morning and evening, and even when he was talking to others, whether they were friends or opponents. It came all of a sudden and went just as suddenly. It lasted for only a very brief period. It was not gradual like lethargy. Furthermore, it was accompanied by those strange noises which were not heard from him or

A Source Beyond Man's World

from anyone else when they went to sleep. This is a condition so unlike that of sleep in all its aspects, times and features. Hence, it is a totally strange condition.

We also find it totally unlike any episode of mental illness or of fits and seizures, for these are normally accompanied by loss of colour, cold limbs, chattering teeth, involuntary exposure of parts which a person would rather remain unseen, and mental black-outs. The difference, as we have seen earlier, is that Muhammad's experience involved increased physical strength, brightness of colour, increased body warmth and resulted in giving light and knowledge. In fact, every time it produced compelling wisdom which the human mind readily accepts.

An External Source

We are nearly there, but we will pause a little to determine the source of this light that appeared occasionally, with the man emanating it having no say as to when it would appear. Could it originate from the nature of Muhammad's soul? If so, it would have been a permanent light that shines all the time, and it would have been more likely to shine when Muhammad was fully alert, or engaged in deep thought, instead of coming only in brief spells when he was under that thin cloud which might have seemed like sleep or loss of consciousness. The inevitable conclusion, then, is that this thin cloud must have had a source of light beyond, which focused on Muhammad's soul every now and then, elevating him to a sublime horizon that transcended his senses, and imparted to him whatever God willed of knowledge. Thereafter, Muhammad returned to his normal state, having acquired knew knowledge that he had not had before. The whole process being repeated time after time.

We all believe that moon light does not emanate from the moon, but is rather a reflection of the sun, because we see that moon light differs all the time according to its position in relation to the sun. In the same way people should believe that the light of this Prophetic moon is a reflection of the light of a sun which remains unseen by them, except for its effects. Indeed, they do not see that sun rising in the day, and they do not hear its voice in clear, understandable speech. However, they have seen an aspect of its light in Muhammad's face and heard its sound near his noble face. This is sufficient as a guiding indication for those who are keen to have such guidance.

It is, then, an external force, because it comes into contact with Muhammad only from time to time. It is, inevitably, a knowledgeable force, because it imparts knowledge. It is higher than him because it has such powerful effects on his body and soul as we have described: *"That is but a Divine inspiration with which he is being inspired, something that a very mighty one has imparted to him: one endowed with surpassing power."* (53: 4-6.)

Moreover, it is a good and noble force that has been made infallible. It inspires only the truth, and orders only what is wise and beneficial. Hence, it has nothing to do with evil forces such as the *jinn* and devils. What access do the *jinn* have to the realm beyond the reach of worldly perception: *"The jinn saw clearly then that, had they but understood the reality which was beyond the reach of their perception, they would not have continued to toil in the shameful suffering."* (34: 14.) Besides, how can the devils have any knowledge of what goes on in the heavens when they have been denied access to them: *"No evil spirits have brought it down: for, neither does it suit their ends, nor is it in their power to [impart it to man]. Indeed they have been utterly debarred even from hearing it."* (26: 210-212.) Besides, spirits are like soldiers who remain together when they are on the same side and move apart when they have nothing in common. A man is known by the company he keeps, and birds of a feather flock together. How can evil spirits be in contact with Muhammad's clearly pure heart, or with his sagacious and perfect mind? *"Shall I tell you upon whom it is that those evil spirits descend? They descend upon all sinful, great liars who eagerly listen [to what the evil spirits say], and most of them are certainly liars."* (26: 221-223.)

A Source Beyond Man's World

What could this force be other than a noble angel?

This is all that we can say about that imperceptible source on a clear and rational basis. A content believer does not need more than this to satisfy his own scientific curiosity, or to reaffirm his faith. Anyone who needs further description of this angelic power and wants more information about its nature should not seek it through logic and reason. He should seek it through what has been authentically reported of the statements of the man who received the light brought by that angelic power, i.e. the Prophet Muhammad (peace be upon him). He is the only one who can give us first hand information about the angel who came to him, and whom he saw with his own eyes and heard with his ears. Indeed, he sat with him on many occasions as a student sits with his tutor.

A person who has no qualms about believing in what lies beyond the reach of human perception, i.e. *ghayb*, will accept such information about the angel Gabriel even though he himself cannot see him. His acceptance is based on what he sees of the effects of the experience of revelation and on his own belief in the Prophet who has given us that information. On the other hand, ignorant people, who possess limited knowledge pertaining only to the outer surface of this world's life yet think themselves to be in possession of unlimited knowledge encompassing everything in the universe, will deny anything that goes beyond their limited knowledge. They may say, 'It may be some visual condition which made Muhammad think that he saw something where there was nothing to see.' Our response to this is a prayer to God to save us from all types of blindness, whether it be in our eyes or in our minds. We repeat what the Qur'an says: *"[His] eye did not waver, nor yet did it stray."* (53: 17.) Or they would say, 'It may all have been some mental disorder that portrayed to him the meanings of words as clear apparitions, and made him see dreams as if they were real.' We dissociate ourselves from all such crazy thoughts and repeat: *"His heart did not give the lie to what he saw."* (53: 11.)

Those non-believers of old could not accept that a human being could see the angels face to face and speak to them directly. In fact they could not accept that there existed creatures whom they could not see with their own eyes or voices they could not hear. They, thus, wondered how Muhammad was able to see and hear what they could not.

Perhaps we should be more amazed at those who advance such ideas. These might have been plausible in the early days of ignorance, but we have, today, plenty of scientific evidence which can be relied upon to explain the mysteries of the world beyond the reach of our perception. One of the new inventions that may be cited in this connection is the telephone which enables two people at the opposite ends of the world to speak to each other while those sitting with either one can see nothing and hear only some noise similar to that of the buzzing of bees, like that heard near the Prophet's face at the time he received revelations.

They may still want even clearer scientific evidence which brings the phenomenon of revelation closer to their minds. They ask to be shown by controlled experiment, which is to them the only basis of certainty, that a link between the human soul and a higher power may produce the same effect, imparting to it information of which it had no previous knowledge, either through physical experience or mental perception. This is clearly seen today in hypnotism where a person of stronger mental power can impose his will over someone weaker than him, placing him in deep slumber during which he does not even feel the prick of needles. The hypnotized person remains under the influence of the stronger person, doing his bidding. He has no will of his own. Should the hypnotist want the person he has hypnotized to forget an opinion or a belief then he can do so. In fact, he can give him a new name which the other person will accept as his own, forgetting all about his real name. He will have the new name, responding when he is called by it and stating that it is his own name. If one man can do this to another, what can be done to man by a much stronger being?

A Source Beyond Man's World

This is a true analogy of the one bringing down the revelation and the one receiving it (peace be upon them both). What we have in this process is a willing human being, with a clear heart and soul, ready to receive all new information imprinted on his mind. The other is a mighty angel endowed with surpassing power, bringing him his message and teaching it to him in such a way that he forgets nothing of it, except as God wills.[4]

But there is a world of difference between the revelation received by God's Messenger and the way people inspire one another. People may, indeed, whisper to one another some dazzling half-truths meant to delude the mind. It is often the case that such whisperings or revelations may end up in giving the receiver some mental or physical disorders that are very difficult to cure. This, however, is very different from revelation transmitted between two empowered messengers whom God has chosen to convey His message: one is an angel and the other a human being. The angel messenger brings nothing but the truth, and orders nothing but goodness. The human messenger, on the other hand, remains after the revelation like he was before it: strong, fully possessed of his exceptional mental strength, and in full command of his physical power. *"God knows best on whom to bestow His message."* (6: 124.)

A Prelude to the Study of a Unique Book

Our method of investigation concerning the source of the Qur'an and how it came to be preached by the Prophet Muhammad (peace be upon him) has so far refrained from tackling the Qur'an in its nature and substance. All that we have done is to study the route it has come through. We have found in the statements of its bearer, his moral values and discipline, his scientific

---

4- This provides further evidence to disprove the claim that it is all a matter of 'self-inspiration' which is advanced by atheists. One essential element to make hypnotism possible is that it be between two widely different natures, one of them stronger than the other. Self hypnotism cannot be administered unless we assume that two opposites can meet within the same soul, or that one entity can be two.

means and sources, as well as his public and private circumstances much accumulating evidence confirming that no one on earth could be described as the author of the Qur'an. Its author is none other than God.

Our study so far has been external. It is perhaps satisfactory for a person who has learnt some of the circumstances of the Prophet's life and manners. Such a person should have at the same time a sound nature, recognising matters for what they really are and linking like with like in order to arrive at the right conclusions. Such a person will be satisfied with what we have said and accept the truth that the Qur'an is God's revelation.

Yet many are those whose knowledge of the Prophet's life is scanty. Such people do not accept the self-evident argument which the Qur'an provides for its author. With these we must move further to show them that by its very nature, the Qur'an cannot have been authored by a human being. It has a very eloquent appeal confirming its being the message of the Almighty. If someone finds a copy of it left in the desert and reads it carefully, without having ever known anything about it, he would realise that it has no worldly origin and that it does not belong to any author on the face of the earth. It originates on high, and from on high it was sent down.

Wide ranging as human ability is, it remains within certain limits beyond which it cannot extend itself, while the power of the Creator is limitless. Everything that goes beyond the ability of mankind remains within God's ability; there is no doubt of this. There is no other situation. Examples of this fact abound. A man may be able to physically overcome another man or two men, or several men, but no single man can stand up to a whole army or nation. God causes the sun to rise in the east. Can anyone cause it to rise in the west? Anyone of us can switch the light on and off at will. But can all mankind bring the sun out before its time, or hold it beyond its setting time, or switch off its light, or come out with a similar sun, even though they harness all their physical and mental powers to achieve that purpose?

5   A Source Beyond Man's World

They certainly cannot create as much as a fly, even if they were to join all their forces to that end. If a fly robs them of anything, they are unable even to rescue it from him. How can they produce something to match those superior objects in the great universe, when they cannot reach them with their hands or even with their missiles? All they can do is to look with admiration at these objects, make use of them and be influenced by them.

This total inability to come up with anything similar to God's creation is an irrefutable proof that it is the work of no human being. It is this Divine quality that distinguishes the work of the Creator from anything that people can make which is the criterion we wish to apply to the Qur'an.

There are people, however, who remain as stubborn as a brick wall. Such are the ones who said to their prophets: *"Whatever sign you may produce before us, with which you aim to cast a spell upon us, we shall not believe you."* (7: 132.) The Qur'anic description of such people goes like this: *"Even if We were to send down angels to them, and if the dead were to speak to them, and even if We were to assemble before them, face to face, all the things [that can prove the truth], they would still not believe unless God so wills."* (6:111.) There are others who are given to doubt. They cannot find their peace in a situation of certainty. They say: *"We think it is no more than an empty guess, and so we are by no means convinced."* (45: 32.) *"If We opened for the non-believers a gateway to heaven and they had ascended higher and higher, still they would surely say: 'It is only our eyes that are spellbound! Indeed, we must have been bewitched.'"* (15: 14-15.) *"If We had sent down to you a writing on paper, and they had touched it with their own hands, the disbelievers would still say, 'This is clearly nothing but deception.'"* (6: 7.)

With neither group can we make any headway. Our counsel is of no benefit to them if God wishes to let them go astray. It is not in our power to make the deaf hear or the blind see. Indeed, we cannot reach out to those who put their fingers in their ears so that they do not hear, or put their hands over their eyes so that they do not see the sun rising up in the middle of the sky. *"If God wills to let anyone to be tempted to evil, you can be of no help to him against God's will.*" (5: 41.) All we can do is set the argument clear to anyone who wishes to know the truth. We only indicate the way to those who wish to travel along.

We call on anyone who truly wishes to arrive at the truth to look with us at the Qur'an from any angle he chooses, its literary style, or the information it provides, or its impact on the history of the world, or from all these angles together. He will then be free to look at it within the constraints of the period of time and social environment in which it appeared, or to assume that it appeared in the most advanced period in history. It is also the same to us if he takes into account the personality of the man who brought it or attributes the Qur'an to an imaginary personality that combines all the adeptness of the best literary talents, the authority of leaders, and the total sum of research made by the best scientists across all branches of science. We will then ask him if he finds in the Qur'an anything less than a unique surpassing power, compared to which the strength of all scientists, leaders, poets and authors dwindle into insignificance. Besides, the world will come to its appointed end while the Qur'an's glitter remains a source of admiration to all. Indeed, life may end before people can grasp its whole truth: "*On the day when its final meaning is unfolded, those who had previously been oblivious to it will say: 'The messengers of Our Lord have indeed told us the truth.'*" (7: 53.)

We will now embark on the study of these three aspects of the unique nature of the Qur'an and its surpassing excellence: the literary, the scientific, and the moral and social. We will concentrate more on its literary and linguistic excellence, because this is where the challenge was thrown to mankind in substance and detail.

Chapter 6

The Qur'an: A Literary Miracle

We seek clarification from anyone who has the slightest doubt that the Qur'an is a miraculous piece of linguistic and literary excellence. We ask such a person why he entertains such doubts. Has he ever thought himself capable of producing a masterpiece of equal literary excellence? Does he acknowledge his inability to do so but assumes that other people may be able to produce what he cannot? Is he fully aware that nobody has ever produced a book of equal literary value to the Qur'an? Does he accept that this is the result of their inability to achieve such a feat or does he believe that their inability is due to the unique nature of the Qur'an itself? Does he know that it is the Qur'an, itself, that placed them in this position of inability, because of its own unique style? Does he recognise that the Qur'an has always been, and still is, a miracle defying all people to produce anything similar to it, and that that includes the person who brought it to us? Or is he convinced of all this, but does not know the reasons for it all?

These, then, represent six different situations, and we have a separate answer for each. We will outline our answers in the same order.

The Qur'an: A Literary Miracle

Aspirations Shattered

It may be such a person's doubts arise from the fact that he has tried his hand at poetry or literary writing, and has found that he has good ability in both. Perhaps his conceit as also his ignorance of the true literary value of the Qur'an has deluded him into thinking that he can produce something of similar excellence. If so, we have a surprise for him. Such thoughts are never entertained by anyone of accomplished and proven literary talent. It occurs only to young upstarts who are yet to prove their merit. We have one piece of advice to give to such a person. Make a formal study, in depth, of all Arabic literary styles. In this way, he will equip himself with sound critical ability, and realise what is needed to judge literary works, and their excellence or otherwise.

When he has done this, let him take a fresh look at the Qur'an. We assure him that every step he takes in this pursuit will increase his appreciation of his own ability and remove more of his doubts about the Qur'an. What he will realise is that the more he knows of literary refinements, and the more adept he is at producing fine speech and excellent style, the readier he is to admit his own weakness and to submit to the superb excellence of the Qur'an. This may sound odd. How is it possible that an increase in knowledge and a fine polishing of acknowledged talent leads to an increased conviction of personal weakness and incompetence?

There is, however, nothing peculiar about this. It applies to everything of God's making. The more you know about what God has created, and the deeper you go in understanding their superb nature, the more ready you are to acknowledge their incomparability and the inability of man to produce anything similar. Different indeed is everything human beings do. A good knowledge of what we humans can achieve will enable you to produce something similar to them and put you on the way to improving them. When we bear this in mind we understand why the magicians in Pharaoh's court were the first to declare their belief in God, the Lord worshipped by Moses and Aaron. They realised that what they were facing was nothing of man's doing but rather the superior power of God Almighty. This they could not challenge.

A person given to arrogance may stubbornly refuse to acknowledge his inability to produce anything similar to the Qur'an. We challenge such a person to have a try and produce for us the best that he can compose so that he may prove his talent and then allow us to judge his claims. But here we have another word of advice for him. He will do well not to show his work until he has considered it very carefully, and reviewed it thoroughly. He must be absolutely certain that he has produced his best. For this will give him a better chance of recognising his mistake and covering up his error. Otherwise, he will only injure himself.

There are several examples in history telling us about those people who made similar attempts. What they produced resembled neither the Qur'an nor their own style. In fact, they were so manifestly flawed and inferior as to rebound on their authors. Some of them soon recognised that it would be much wiser if they ceased their efforts. They folded their parchments and broke their pens. Those who were more cunning realised that people were too wise to accept their false inventions and hence they hid them for a time. A third type did not hesitate to publish their work, earning people's ridicule. Whoever may think of trying his hand at this should look at these examples and choose the best practice to follow. But a person who has no sense of shame will continue to do what he likes.

Among the first type, the names of Ibn Al-Muqaffaᶜ, Al-Mutanabbi and Al-Maᶜarri should be mentioned here. These were men of letters and each, undoubtedly, possessed great talent. Hence, we believe that these exercised sufficiently wise judgements and fine literary tastes to preclude the possibility that any of them would make such an attempt, unless such an attempt aimed at satisfying themselves that the Qur'an is inimitable.

Among the second type we may cite the books produced by the founders of the Qadiani and Bahaii creeds. These are meant to provide a religious constitution for their followers to implement. In essence, however, they

The Qur'an: A Literary Miracle

are no more than a fabricated mess in which they employ some Qur'anic verses coupled with a plethora of slang. In them, they distort some of the fundamentals of Islam as also some of its details. They also claim prophethood or even divinity for themselves. Nevertheless, their followers could not publish their falsehoods at a time when standards of literary education were high. Therefore, they concealed them in the hope that a time would come when ignorance was far more commonplace. They realised that only at such a time could they market their merchandise. Well, they may have to wait to the end of human life on earth before their ambitions are realised.

The best example of the third type was Musaylamah, an impostor who claimed that he was a messenger of God. He was a contemporary of the Prophet Muhammad, and he alleged that he received revelations similar to the Qur'an. But all he did was to extrapolate verses from the Qur'an, retaining most of their wordings whilst changing others. He also retained the rhythm of the Qur'an, but used a number of slang words to express a host of stupid meanings. An Arab living at a time of high literary standards as he was, he could not maintain his own style. He went so low as to produce something similar to what children do when they change the words of songs and poems to give them different meanings. Needless to say, this is no more than distorting the work of others. A person who seriously wishes to take up the challenge to produce something similar to the Qur'an should take a particular idea expressed in the Qur'an, then express it in a different style of equal or greater merit to that of the Qur'anic text. Anyone who wishes to try this with the ideas of the Qur'an will only try what is impossible. Experience provides irrefutable proof. In fact, anyone who tries to express other ideas in a style similar to that of the Qur'an, without confining himself to what is true and wise, will see that his efforts are fruitless. Hence why the Qur'anic challenge to the Arabs required them to produce ten surahs similar to the Qur'an, but *'invented by yourselves'*. (11: 13.)

We endorse what al-Rāfiʿi, a contemporary authority on literature, believes regarding that which Musaylamah produced. He says that Musaylamah did not wish to produce anything of similar literary merit. It was clear to him that that was impossible. Moreover, the result would be only too clear to the Arabs. He simply wanted to win favour with his own people, playing on their weaknesses. He realised that in pre-Islamic days the Arabs held monks in high esteem. Since monks produced rhyming phrases that they attributed to the *jinn*, he resorted to the same style in imitating the Qur'an. He hoped to delude his people into believing that, like Muhammad, he also received revelations, thus equating being a prophet with being a monk. Even in this he was unsuccessful. Many of his followers were aware that he was a liar devoid of wisdom. They acknowledged that as a monk, he fared very poorly, and as a prophet he was a downright liar. Yet they followed him because to them, 'The liar from the Rabīʿah tribe is dearer than the truthful man from the Muḍar tribe.'

A Work of Inimitable Merit

A person's doubt may be based on his recognition that there are others who possess exceptional literary merit. He may well think, 'If I, personally, am not the right one to take up such a challenge, the task may be better addressed by one who is better in speech and finer in literary skills.' We advise such a person to ask those who are recognised as having the best literary talent in his age whether or not they are able to imitate the Quan and produce a literary piece of a similar standard. If they answer that it should not be too difficult for them, we will ask them to prove their claim. If, on the other hand, they admit their inability to do so, we say that such an admission is the best proof.

Let us then look back in history wondering if anyone was ever equal to the task. History will tell us that never did anyone stand up to the Qur'an in a competition of excellence. The few individuals who attempted anything of the sort were soon to end their attempts recognising their utter failure. None of them managed to achieve a position of even moderate fame.

The Qur'an: A Literary Miracle

Indeed, history records that the Arabs themselves failed to produce anything like the Qur'an even in the same period of its revelation, which is universally recognised as the time of their highest linguistic abilities and their finest literary achievements. No language or literary academy anywhere in the world took as much care of its language as the Arabs did during that period of time. In fact, it was then that Arabic attained its most superb standards in vocabulary and stylistic refinements. They held special, regularly organised fairs for their best products, masterpieces made of nothing other than letters and words. Their merchandise nothing more than poems and speeches, which they exhibited, competing for honour and high position. Both men and women were amongst the competitors, those of the calibre of Ḥassān ibn Thābit and Al-Khansā' who are well known to any student of Arabic literature. [It should be remembered here that there is no contradiction between the Arabs being illiterate, in the sense that they had no formal education and could not, except for a few of their number, read and write, and the fact that many of them had natural literary gifts which enabled them to compose poetry of the highest standard.]

But when the Qur'an was revealed all such fairs came to an end, and literary gatherings were defunct. From now on, the Qur'an was the only work to command people's attention. None of them could challenge or compete with it, or even suggest that a single word be changed, moved, added or omitted from the sentence where it occurs. Yet the Qur'an did not close the door to competition. Indeed, it left it wide open, calling on them, individually and collectively, to take up its challenge and produce anything similar to it. It repeated the challenge in different forms, berating their inability to do so, and reducing the task for them time after time. It required them first to come up with a similar book, then asked them to produce ten surahs like it, then one surah only, then it asked them to produce a surah comparable to it; i.e. a surah which resembled the Qur'an in one way or another, as if to say: 'You are only asked to produce something that bears some similarities, vague as they may be, to the Qur'an.' This is indeed the lowest level to which such a challenge can be reduced. Hence, chronologically, this was the last challenge to be made, as it occurs in Surah 2, which was revealed in Madinah. The previous challenges all occur in the Makkan revelations. This is a subtle, but important difference.

The challenge, however, goes further than this. Each time, they are expressly allowed to seek the help of anyone they care to call in for support. It then tells them in the most emphatic way that they will still be totally incapable of meeting the challenge: *"If all mankind, and all the jinn, would come together with a view to producing the like of this Qur'an, they would not produce its like even though they were to exert all their strength in aiding one another."* (17: 88.) *"If you are in doubt regarding what We have bestowed from on high upon Our servant [Muhammad], then produce a surah comparable to it, and call upon anyone other than God to bear witness for you, if what you say is true. And if you cannot do it - and most certainly you cannot do it - then be conscious of the Fire whose fuel is human beings and stones which awaits those who reject the truth."* (2: 23-24.)

Consider this challenge carefully and look at how provocatively it is expressed. It states a final verdict of total failure at all times: *"And most certainly you cannot do it."* It then threatens them with the Fire and puts them in the same position as stones. Had they had even the slightest chance of meeting the challenge, they would not have held back, considering that they were its avowed enemies who were known to be always ready to defend their honour. Here, the Qur'an hits out at their pride and honour. But still they could not find even a way to compete with it. They simply found themselves at the bottom of a high mountain with absolutely no means of climbing it. When they realised their total inability to produce anything similar to the Qur'an, the only answer they had was to resort to arms instead of letters, and to risk their lives instead of their literary talents. This is, indeed, the resort of anyone who has no argument to present, knowing that he stands on shallow ground, and that he cannot justify his position with pen and paper, or with speech and argument.

The Qur'an: A Literary Miracle

The revelation of the Qur'an was then completed, with the challenge still standing for anyone who wanted to try. This period of time was followed by one when the edges of the Arabian desert were still inhabited by a people who maintained their purity of race and language. These enjoyed an intrinsic ability to appreciate fine style and literary expression. Among them were people who would not have hesitated for a minute if they could undermine the very foundation of the religion of Islam. Had they been able, in any way, to improve upon their predecessors and produce anything that competed with the Qur'an for literary merit, they would not have had a moment's hesitation. Instead, they continued to hang down their heads in recognition of their utter failure. In fact, a barrier was set between them and what they desired, as was the case with their predecessors.

Generations followed generations, and the Arabic language passed on to new folk. However, the latter have been even more powerless to meet this lasting challenge. They have recognised that they are no match for it. Their own admission is added to the testimony history gives of their predecessors. The proof of their inability is two fold: a conscious realisation and a rational argument proving that no one can ever produce anything similar to the Qur'an. This will remain true to the end of time.

Anyone to Take up the Challenge?

Some people may acknowledge that no one has ever produced anything like the Qur'an, but that does not mean that such an objective lies beyond human ability. Anyone may simply choose not to do something either because he does not like doing it, or because there is no motivating reason, or because something beyond his own control has diverted his attention or weakened his resolve despite adequate motivation, or it may be that an unexpected event interfered with his means or ability to do it after he had resolved to do so. The two first situations indicate that people did not produce anything like the Qur'an because they did not care to do so, rather than as a result of their inability. The third situation indicates a disability to complete the task, not because of any excellence that places the Qur'an beyond human ability, but because of the intervention of an external power. Such an intervention by the Supreme Power [i.e. God] aims to protect the Qur'an from contention and competition. If this barrier were to be removed, people would be able to produce something similar to the Qur'an, or so the argument contends. This view was advanced by al-Niẓām of the Muʿtazilah school of philosophy. Although it admits the inimitability of the Qur'an, this argument can only be advanced by a non-Arab or someone who has no literary taste. This explains why even his student, al-Jāḥiẓ, a famous Arab literary figure, did not follow al-Niẓām's view. Nor did any one conversant with the Arabic language and literature. It is contrary to what the Arabs accept.

None of these situations applies to our present discussion. As for the first situation, we say that the motives for producing something with which to challenge the Qur'an were too strong to ignore. What motivates an opponent more than your repeated challenge and ridicule, in which you declare that, try as he may, he can in no way produce anything similar to your own work? Such ridicule is sufficient to motivate even a coward to muster his strength, to rise and defend himself. What effect, then, would it have on a person known for guarding his honour and defending his position? What if you are challenging him over something in which he is particularly adept and in which he takes exceptional pride? What if you couple your challenge by accusing him of following erroneous ideas and false concepts? And what would be his attitude when he realises that your aim behind all this verbal warfare is to demolish his faith and to cause a split between his future and his past?

As for the second situation, we see here that there were strong reasons motivating opponents to the extreme. In fact, the position of Muhammad and the Qur'an he recited was their top preoccupation. They resorted to every possible method of opposition, whether peaceful or violent. They even sought to appease him so that he would give in a little and reduce his

The Qur'an: A Literary Miracle

opposition to their religion.[5] Furthermore, they offered him money and the position of a king[6] if only he would stop his message. On the other hand, they made a solemn pact agreeing to boycott him and his clan until they all perished or until his clan surrendered him to them[7] so that they could kill him. They tried hard to prevent the voice of the Qur'an when it was recited by Muslims, so that it was not heard by their sons or womenfolk.[8] They also waged a smear campaign against the Prophet, accusing him of being a sorcerer, or a madman, hoping by so doing to prevent him from influencing any pilgrims that might visit Makkah. They also plotted to imprison or kill him or to send him into exile, as the Qur'an reports: *"The unbelievers were scheming against you, in order to restrain you, or to kill you, or to drive you away."* (8: 30.) They even went to war repeatedly against him, risking their lives and putting their families to much hardship.

Was all this a mark of their being preoccupied with something else to the extent that they could not be bothered to produce something as powerful as the Qur'an? Moreover, why would they go to all this trouble when he had told them time and again that the only way to silence him was to produce something similar to the revelation he brought them? This seems to be the proper and easier way out for them, had they been able to do it. The fact

---

5- Some people from the Quraysh, the Prophet's tribe, came to him and said: 'Muhammad, if you will pay your respects to our deities, we will accept your faith. God revealed in the Qur'an: *"They endeavour to tempt you away from all the truth with which We have inspired you."* (17: 73.)

6- A group of the Quraysh leaders also came to the Prophet offering to make him the richest person in Arabia or to make him their king, if only he would abandon his message.

7- This refers to the covenant in which the Quraysh pledged themselves to boycott Muhammad and his clan, making no trade and initiating no marital or social relationships with them unless they surrendered the Prophet to them.

8- Abu Bakr, the Prophet's closest Companion used to recite the Qur'an in his own yard, and some young men, women and slaves were impressed by what they heard. The Quraysh leaders feared that some of them might become Muslims. They asked Ibn al-Dughunnah, Abu-Bakr's protector, to withdraw his protection unless Abu Bakr agreed to read the Qur'an indoors where he could not be heard.

remains that they resorted to every method except this one. Sacrificing their lives, risking being taken captive, and suffering poverty and humiliation were much easier for them than the alternative which he had indicated to them. But they found this extremely difficult, indeed impossible. Hence, their total powerlessness.

The whole campaign of opposition was not directed against the Prophet and his Companions in person. There were family and tribal bonds between the two sides, and the high moral standards the Muslims upheld earned them much respect, even among the non-believers. Nor was the campaign launched against the Qur'an when a person learns it by heart and recites it at home. The Quraysh non-believers were prepared to accept that everyone was free to worship their Lord at home as they wished. Instead, this whole campaign was directed at achieving one single goal, namely preventing the propagation of the Qur'an among the rest of the Arabs. This is clearly indicated by the Prophet when he approached different tribes requesting them to protect him in his endeavour to make his message known to mankind. He would say to them: "Would you be prepared to take me to your quarters, for the Quraysh have prevented me from conveying the message of my Lord." [Related by Abu Dāwūd and al-Tirmidhi.]

We must not imagine for a moment that their opposition to publicising the Qur'an was based merely on the fact that it preached a new faith. There were among them a number of highly endowed poets and speakers who did not indulge in idolatry, such as Quss ibn Sāʿidah and Umayyah ibn Abi al-Salt, who included in their speeches and poems much of the moral values advocated in the Qur'an. But they did not give such advocates of moral values the same attention as they gave the Qur'an. Nor were they bothered or concerned with their preaching. The fact is that they felt that the Qur'an was different from any other type of speech. Its argument was overpowering. It removed everything that stood in its way and imposed its authority wherever it reached. They could not even stand up to it in a way they were undoubtedly adept at, which was to produce something of equal

The Qur'an: A Literary Miracle

merit and power. Since this was the subject matter of the challenge put to them, then the only way to resist it was to suppress it by all means, making any sacrifice required to ensure that. This was indeed their policy, and it has been the policy of all enemies of the Qur'an ever since.

The third situation supposes that an external cause prevented them from producing what they needed, and had the ability, to produce, i.e. a piece of equal merit. Had this been true, they would not have recognised their inability until they so tried. No one feels unable to do something that he is used to doing as easily as sitting and standing, until he has tried it at least once. But we know that they did not even try to produce anything similar to the Qur'an. The only ones to even make an attempt were a few individuals who were amongst the least wise of them. This indicated an instinctive recognition that their inability to accomplish this task was total, just like their inability to move mountains, or to reach out to the stars. It is this recognition that was behind their lack of effort.

Had they not been aware, right from the outset, of their inability to produce anything similar to the Qur'an, they would certainly have made a determined effort to meet the challenge. This would have meant that they might initially have felt that it was of the same standard as their own speech. But after their failure to produce anything similar to the Qur'an, they would have wondered at this incidental inability on their part, how they were held back when they were always otherwise able to meet a challenge. They would have asked themselves, 'What is the matter with us that we are unable to match the Qur'an which is like our normal speech?' Or they would have resorted to their finest literary works produced prior to this unexpected inability, and delivered from them something similar to the Qur'an. But they failed to produce anything, whether old or new. The Qur'an, itself, was their constant source of wonder and their centre of admiration. They would even prostrate themselves in submission to God, its author, when they heard it, before they even had had time to reflect. Some of them candidly acknowledged: "This could not have been said by any human being."

New Material from Old Fabric

A person may say: I accept that people have not managed to come up with anything similar to the Qur'an because they are incapable of doing so. They may have found in the Qur'an something of a miraculous nature that puts it beyond their reach. But I cannot understand that the linguistic aspect can be part of the secret in the Qur'anic miracle. When I read the Qur'an I find that it is not different from the language of the Arabs. Its words are composed of their own sounds, letters and alphabet, and its verses and sentences use the same words they use, and, indeed, it follows their own modes of expression. The Qur'anic vocabulary has the same roots and methods of derivation as the Arabs use in their language. The construction of its sentences comes in patterns that have always been familiar to the Arabs. How can you say, then, that the Qur'an confronts them with something beyond the reach of their linguistic ability?

In reply we acknowledge that, in vocabulary and construction, the Qur'an follows the same pattern as the Arabic language has always used. This is undoubtedly true. But it is this that makes its challenge clearer, leaving no room for excuses: *"Had We willed to express this Qur'an in a non-Arabic tongue, they would surely have said, 'Why is it that its verses have not been spelled out clearly? Why [a message in] a non-Arabic tongue, and [its bearer] an Arab?'"* (41: 44.)

But are we not ignoring here the basic similarity between literature and architecture? An architect does not come up with a building material that is not available on earth. Nor do architects steer away from the basic rules of their profession. What they do is no more than raise walls, lay floors and ceilings, and put up doors, windows and gates. But the quality of their work varies a great deal, depending on the choice of the best and longer-lasting material, giving residents protection against extreme heat and cold. They choose how deep to lay their foundations and how high to make their buildings, how to make the load lighter for the supporting parts, how to make the best use of the space provided in order to accommodate more facilities,

6. The Qur'an: A Literary Miracle

how to arrange the interior so as to bring light and ventilation to all rooms and halls. Some of them may achieve all this, or most of it, while others may have one or more defects. Then they add decoration of wide-ranging variety according to taste and personal choice.

In the same way, people of the same language may express the same meaning in different ways with varying degrees of excellence and acceptability. Yet none of these goes beyond the vocabulary or the grammatical rules [i.e. the basic material] of their language. It is the talented choice of the material they use that elevates their speech to the extent that it attracts audiences and generates enchantment and admiration. Conversely, vulgar choice may make it totally unattractive to the extent that it jars on people's ears and causes them to turn away in disgust.

In its great variety of expression, a language uses different constructions and styles, such as the general and the peculiar, the restricted and the unrestricted, the concise and the detailed. It spells out things, or it may point or refer to them in general terms or even implicitly. It uses reporting or statement forms, nominal or verbal sentences, negation and confirmation, fact and allegory, verbose and concise styles. It may spell out certain things or delete them leaving only an implied reference to them, and it may give a sentence an abrupt start or may use a conjunction. It uses nouns with definite or indefinite articles, and it uses inversion, putting words ahead of, or later than, their usual place. In their speech and writings people may use any combination of these forms and modes of expression to convey the meanings they have in mind. In none of these, however, do they go beyond the framework of the language. In fact, they take their own routes within its limits and they confine themselves within its boundaries.

Yet none of these various forms and modes befits every situation, and none is deemed unsuitable to all. Were that the case, the matter would be easy for everyone. Fine style would impart the same taste to all, sounding the same tune in all ears. The same route may lead you to the place you are heading on one occasion, but may prove to be the wrong way on others. A word may seem to be the missing jewel in a certain situation, while it has no particular significance in another. This means that the choice of style depends on the meaning a person wishes to convey and certainty that it is the best way to convey it accurately. If you are involved in an argument, you want to choose a style that presents your case clearly, leaving no room for ambiguity. If you are presenting a description, you need a style that is more accurate in outlining details. In a friendly situation you choose what people find easy and gentle, while in a dispute you may need what is strong and uncompromising. In all situations, we look for what expresses our purpose more clearly and is likely to retain its appeal for a long time to come.

Such a choice is by no means easy, because the variety on offer is great indeed, using a wide range of colours and styles in vocabulary and construction. People do not have the same ability to examine all these styles, let alone make an informed choice between them. One person may hit on something that eludes another, while each may remain unaware of the other's choice. A form you miss here may be equal to two you use there, and vice versa.

All the elements that a person observes when he speaks combine to generate a special picture bringing together certain mental constituents. It is similar to the 'mode' in material constituents. This mode of speech is what we call style. It is in style that people differ in their speech and its degree of excellence and acceptability.

What is new in the language of the Qur'an is that in every purpose the Qur'an tackles, it selects the best material and the closest to the meaning intended, bringing together all required shades that can readily be mixed together. It puts every little element in its most suitable and fitting place. Its meaning is reflected superbly in its words, as if the words return a mirror image depicting its complete and true picture. To a word, its meaning is its secure home where it is permanently settled. The home does not look for a different dweller, and the resident does not aspire for a better home. The Qur'anic style gives you this perfect example of literary excellence.

The Qur'an: A Literary Miracle

Proof of this is in abundance, but we will not look into such evidence now. We will come to it later. We are only concentrating for the present on the point that not all Arabic speech is the same. Linguistic and literary excellence may sink to the point of total inadequacy or may rise to a most sublime standard defying all imitation.

If someone wishes to look for proof of the Qur'anic excellence in this respect, when he is not qualified to be a judge of literary styles, then he has to realise that only through a fine sense and a wealth of experience can judgement be fair. Hence, his only alternative is to accept the verdict of other people and to be content with the testimony of those who are qualified to so return one. Therefore, it is pertinent to give here one such testimony.

Al-Walīd ibn al-Mughīrah was one of the chiefs of the Quraysh tribe in Makkah. He came once to talk to the Prophet, but the Prophet read a passage of the Qur'an to him. It seems that al-Walīd softened his hostile attitude to the Prophet as a result. When Abu Jahl, the most unyielding opponent of Islam among the Quraysh, heard of this, he went to al-Walīd and said: "Uncle, your people are collecting some money to give you, because you went to Muhammad seeking what he may have to give you." Al-Walīd replied: "The Quraysh is aware that I am among the richest people here." Abu Jahl suggested: "Then you have to say something about him which would indicate to your people that you are hostile to him." Al-Walīd said: "What can I say? There is none among you who is a better judge of poetry, with all its forms and styles, including the poetry said by the *jinn*, than me. By God, what Muhammad says is nothing like any of that. What he says has its own sweetness and refinement. It is all light at the top, shining at the bottom. It is surpassing, overpowering. Nothing can stand up to it." Abu Jahl insisted: "Your people will not be satisfied until you have said something against it." Al-Walīd asked for time to think, and when he had finished his thinking he said: "This is sorcery that he has learnt from someone else."

In response to this, the following verses were revealed to the Prophet: *"Leave Me to deal with him whom I have created alone, and to whom I have granted vast resources, and children as [love's] witnesses, and to whose life I gave so wide a scope; and yet, he greedily desires that I give yet more! No, indeed. It is against Our revelations that he knowingly, stubbornly sets himself. So I shall constrain him to endure a painful uphill climb! Behold, [when Our revelations are conveyed to him,] he reflects and meditates - and thus he destroys himself, the way he meditates. Yes, indeed, he destroys himself, the way he meditates! Then he looks around [for new arguments], and then he frowns and glares, and in the end he turns his back and glories in his arrogance, and says, 'All this is mere spellbinding eloquence handed down to him [from olden times]! This is nothing but the word of mortal human beings."* (74: 11-25.)

Consider for a moment how the Qur'an describes how hard the man labours in order to reach his final verdict on the Qur'an: He reflects and meditates, looking around for argument, frowning and glaring, turning his back and behaving most arrogantly. All this shows how he struggles with his own nature, trying to come up with a verdict that his own conscience is bound to disapprove of. This constrained him no end. Yet finally, he had to succumb to his people's desire and return a hostile verdict. Consider also the wide gulf between this arbitrary verdict and the one that comes naturally from the same person when he expresses his opinion freely: "It is surpassing, overpowering. Nothing can stand up to it".

That is a final testimony for anyone who does not have the qualification to distinguish styles and judge literary expression. Sufficient to say that it is a testimony given by one who knows, a person from among the people whose native language was the language of the Qur'an. And yet he was as hostile to Islam as its hardest enemies.

On the other hand, if you are qualified to judge styles and distinguish literary excellence, then all you have to do is to read whatever you wish of speeches, poetry, epistles, proverbs, dialogues, fiction and non-fiction, from pre-Islamic days to the present. Then take any page of the Qur'an and consider what you find there.

The Qur'an: A Literary Miracle

You will find a remarkable style and a unique mode of expression. It is as if all other styles are very familiar, while among them it, the Qur'an, stands out in a unique position. You will not find anything similar to it in what earlier literary figures had composed. Nor did a latter day literary genius produce anything akin to it in any way. If a verse of the Qur'an is given in the midst of a rich collection of what the most eloquent people have composed in speech or writing, it will stand out prominently. It will be readily distinguished, just like a fine tune will stand out among what may be described as 'run of the mill', or like a fresh ripening fruit among different types of food.

Miraculous Even to the Message Preacher

Someone may say at this point that we have addressed one type of doubt but opened another. He may even go back to what we have said about how literary styles differ a great deal, and how people may achieve varying degrees of excellence in their modes of expression. His argument may run in the following fashion. Since literary expression varies among people, then literary excellence is accessible to all people, and we find it in all sorts of writings and speech, as we find it in the Qur'an. Indeed, every speaker and writer puts into his style something of his mind and conscience, in the form his talent chooses. Since people have different talents and experiences, their styles differ when they express their thoughts.

In fact, we can count as many forms of Arabic speech as there are Arabic native speakers. It is impossible to find two writers or speakers using exactly identical styles. Every one has his or her own method of expression. A bedouin is unlike a city dweller, an intelligent person is unlike a man of poor intelligence. A rash or an ill person has a different style from that of a wise or healthy person. One of inferior talent cannot rise to a high standard, and one who enjoys a superior talent cannot reach a level well beneath him. Indeed, two people may have very similar modes and natures, and an identical education, yet they may have the same experience but use totally different styles of expression. How do you challenge them to produce something similar to the Qur'an when they cannot produce each other's styles? How do you consider this inability a proof of its Divine source when you do not attribute their inability to imitate each other as indicative of any Divine intervention that gives the speaker no say in what he utters? Indeed, this analogy tells us that the Qur'an is the word of a human being and, in this respect, it is not different from what human beings say or produce. It simply reflects certain characteristics that are applicable to the one who said it in the same way as every literary piece reflects the characteristics of its author.

In reply to the person advancing such an argument we acknowledge that whatever a person says is a product that is influenced by his nature and talents which, as they differ from one person to another, are reflected in different styles and standards. Yet even when such natures and talents are closely similar among a group of people, dictating similar types of speech, still their final products are widely different.

All this we readily accept, but it takes nothing away from our own argument. When we challenge people to produce something similar to the Qur'an, we do not ask them to come up with exactly the same mode and style. This is something we know to be well beyond anyone's reach. What we challenge them to produce is a speech that may take any form or style, in which the speaker, by mode and nature, feels at ease with, provided that such a speech has literary merits that are similar or close to that of the Qur'an. The challenge is concerned with literary merit, which is the field in which men and women of letters compete, attain similar or widely different standards. This is a different issue from that of methods and figures of speech that vary from one speaker to another.

If anyone finds it hard to understand how comparability can be achieved with such difference, we cite the example of athletes running along a track, and each one of them sticking to his lane so that he does not step over the toes of his competitor. They are all following parallel lines, aiming to reach the same point. Yet we find among them one who comes top, and others

The Qur'an: A Literary Miracle

who follow in rank until we have the last who trails them all. Some may run neck and neck. Yet while each maintains his lane, similarity and excellence are easily identified among them, according to how fast they approach their common finishing line.

The same applies to those who compete in literary expression. Each one of them selects the route he wants to follow and the format he wishes to work with in order to achieve the goal he has set for himself. They will show themselves, then, to be either of the same standard or of different standards in as much as they fulfil the requirements of fine literary writings.

Let us suppose that those who are called upon to produce something like the Qur'an include some who are equal to the Prophet, who received the message of the Qur'an, in their native Arabic literary talent, or perhaps some of them have a superior talent. Or let us suppose that they are all of lesser standard than him. Those whose talent is superior should be able to produce something better than what he recited to them, and those who are equal should come up with something similar to it, while the rest should not find it impossible to compose something that has some similarity to it. Anything of any of these three degrees would have been sufficient to refute the argument of the uniqueness of the Qur'an and defeat the challenge posed. Yet the first one is not even mentioned in the Qur'an because the impossibility of the task is taken for granted.

It may be said that it is better to accept that the Arabs, with all their varying talents, could not rise to the standard of Muhammad's superb literary ability. Let us also accept that their recognised inability to come up with something similar to his own speech generally caused them to fall short of trying to imitate the Qur'an. Yet this cannot be used as argument in support of the claim that the Qur'anic style is Divine, just as it has not been used to claim any Divinity for the Prophet's own style.

In reply we say that Muhammad was certainly the most eloquent of all Arabs. His was the top place among them all in literary excellence. This is a fact universally accepted among all who know Arabic and its literary standards. But the question that should be asked here is about the degree of his superiority: is it of the type that is usually seen between human beings in different areas? Or is it totally supernatural?

If it is of the type we normally recognise between a fine style and one that is even finer, or between degrees of beauty, we say that such distinction as he enjoyed would not have precluded them from composing a single piece like it. Even if they found it impossible to achieve the same degree of excellence, they could have achieved a comparable degree. It would have been acceptable for them to produce something similar to the Qur'an, in whole or in part, whether long or short, exactly similar or showing only some aspects of similarity. Nevertheless, their inability to do so has been total.

And if it is said that the difference between Muhammad and all talented experts of fine speech was such that put him on a sublime level to which none can ever rise, because of his unique nature which is totally unlike that of all others, then that is akin to saying that some human beings are superhuman. Indeed, it constitutes an admission that what such a person produces is not the work of any human being. The fact is that all human beings share in what we term generally as human nature. Within that, personal natures exhibit similarities that reveal themselves time after time, in one person after another, at least over different periods, if not during the same period of time. This applies at least to some, if not all aspects of expression. Many are those who have similar thoughts and views, and they express them in similar styles and, at times, use identical phrases and expressions. A reader may even think that the products of such writers have the same feel and aura. This is particularly seen in the works of those who imitate earlier literary figures who had highly distinctive styles.

Had the Qur'an been the work of the human being who conveyed it to us, producing something similar to it would not have been difficult for one who is akin to that person in mood and character, sharing the same values and conducting himself according to his guidance, or to one who is closely

The Qur'an: A Literary Miracle

related to him and who learnt much from him. Indeed, it would have been appropriate for Muhammad's Companions who learnt the Qur'an directly form him, appreciated its excellence, understood and implemented its message and conducted their life in accordance with its guidance to try to make their own styles similar to that of the Qur'an. This would have been the natural response to man's instinctive desire to imitate what he considers to be superior. But nothing of this was attempted. The most that such literary figures tried was to copy an expression here or there to add to the power of their argument or the beauty of their style. The same is done by the best literary talents in our own modern times.

The Prophet's Superior Literary Style

Had the Qur'anic style been a reflection of Muhammad's own nature, that reflection should have shown itself, following the above argument, in everything that Muhammad said. A person's nature cannot be two different natures, nor can a person's soul be two souls. When we consider the Qur'anic style we find it the same throughout, while the Prophet's own style is totally different. It does not run alongside the Qur'an except like high-flying birds which cannot be reached by man but which may 'run' alongside him. When we look at human styles we find them all of a type that remains on the surface of the earth. Some of them crawl while others run fast. But when you compare the fastest running among them to the Qur'an you feel that they are no more than moving cars compared to planets speeding through their orbits.

You may read a piece of the Prophet's own words and you may feel tempted to imitate it, just like a sharp shooter being tempted to drop a flying bird, or a fast runner attempting to keep pace with it. You may, on the other hand, read a wise saying and wonder whether it is part of the Prophet's statements, or if it was said by one of his Companions or their successors [i.e. *Tābiʿīn*]. Yet you know that the Prophet's style is distinguished by superior literary excellence, with its vocabulary best fitting the subject matter it tackles, and this is coupled with fine construction. However, its distinction may not be readily appreciated except by literary experts. Nevertheless, literary sense alone may not be sufficient to appreciate its full excellence immediately. So we may resort to reference books in order to ascertain whether it is directly attributed to the Prophet or its chain of reporting stops at one of the Prophet's Companions or their successors.

The Qur'anic style, on the other hand, has its own distinctive features which make it unlike any other style. No one ever tries to come near it. People may wonder how they can produce something similar to it, but they will soon give up any such attempt.

Anyone who is in full possession of his senses and is endowed with a literary sense and a critical linguistic taste needs only to listen with one ear to the Qur'anic style and with the other to the style of the Prophet's statements [i.e. hadith] and to other people's styles. He will then readily acknowledge the indisputable fact that the style of the Qur'an is far superior to any other. We think that once he has admitted this fact, he will also admit the next one, which considers that a product with nothing similar to it in any way must be the work of the One to whom no similarities apply. That is God, who hears all and sees all.

Perhaps we should add here an objection that may be raised by someone who says that a person may have two types of speech. The first may occur instinctively and is uttered directly, without any refinement. The other is produced after deliberation and careful selection. The difference between the two may be wide indeed, to the extent that a listener may judge that the two types emanate from two different people. Such a person may add that this could be applied to Muhammad's heritage, with the hadith being of the first type and the Qur'an of the second.

In answer we say that classifying the hadith and the Qur'an according to these two types of style does not fit at all with what happened in practice. Most Qur'anic revelations addressed topics the Prophet had not expected.

The Qur'an: A Literary Miracle

He had not thought about them earlier. It would come all of a sudden, without him expecting revelation at all. It may answer a question that had been put to him, or may give a verdict on a particular incident, or may relate something of the history of an earlier community, etc. It rarely addressed a topic on which the Prophet had been looking for some revelation, when exercising care and meticulous refinement was possible, as in the case of the false accusation against his wife and in the change of the direction in prayer. When we consider the Qur'anic style in both these situations we find it of the same nature, construction and excellence.

The same applies to hadith, which was said in different situations and under widely different circumstances, but its style remains the same. The Prophet would speak after long reflection and consultation with his Companions, as happened when he had to deal with the false accusations levelled at his wife, and also when he spoke after the consultations regarding war and peace and other matters. Or he would speak after a short while waiting for revelations to be given to him.

This is clearly seen in the event of a man who came to the Prophet at Al-Ji‘ranah, near Makkah, in year 8 and asked him about the ‘umrah. He had applied much perfume and was wearing a garment. The Prophet looked at him intently and kept silent until he received revelations. When that was over, he enquired: "Where is the man who asked about the ‘umrah?" When the man came over, the Prophet said to him: "As for the perfume, you wash it three times; and as for your garment, take it off and wear for the ‘umrah what you wear for pilgrimage." [Related by al-Bukhari and Muslim.] At times, he spoke directly on matters which were clear, or which had been considered before, whether relating to religion or thought. In all this, his style followed the same pattern. One cannot distinguish a separate or distinct style for that which he had thought about himself, or for that which he had been given by revelation, or for that which he spoke instinctively in his discussions with his family or with his Companions, or for that which he said in speeches he made before large crowds or on great occasions. This shows the fallacy of trying to distinguish the Qur'an from hadith in this way.

Indeed if for argument's sake we accept this division, it would not serve as a basis for doubt. Dividing a person's speech into what is said extempore and what is composed with care and deliberation would not result, among true Arabs, in such a wide difference giving the impression that the two types were said by two different people. Such a wide difference appeared only when true Arabic speakers had died out. They were replaced by people who had not learnt this language from their mothers. Hence, the language they spoke was different from the one they wrote. This gave each of them two different styles, with one sinking to the level of natural dialect and the other elevated to learnt Arabic standards.

A pure native speaker of Arabic at the Prophet's time would have only concentrated on his topic and gathered its different aspects as a result of careful thinking and deliberation. This would not have caused him to change his style, method of expression or his natural language which comes to him without affectation. This sort of style is the one which specialised people among us attempt after study and consideration. Among the Arabs of that time, there might have been a few who would resort to affectation when they spoke, but that affectation would not have taken them completely out of their natural style. There would remain in what they produced some characteristics indicating the type of style they employed. Moreover, affectation would not have improved their standard. On the contrary, it decreased its rank in the scale of excellence, although the speaker might have thought otherwise. In fact, the Arabs used to praise literary style that came to the speaker naturally, without affectation.

The Prophet himself never resorted to affectation in any situation. Indeed, affectation was abhorrent to him in all matters. He used to say: "The pedantic have perished!" [Related by Muslim and Abu Dāwūd]. A man from the tribe of Hudhayl spoke to him about having to pay blood money for causing the death of a foetus, saying: "How is it possible that I should pay money in compensation for one who neither ate nor drank, neither spoke nor cried? That is surely one whose blood is of no value!" The Prophet

The Qur'an: A Literary Miracle

said disapprovingly: "That is the brother of fortune tellers, using rhyme like theirs." His reference to fortune tellers is aimed at the rhyming phrases they used in order to give their prophecies an air of mystery. It was of the type where the meaning is made subservient to the words, not the reverse.

What we have said so far about the wide gulf between the style of the Qur'an and the style of hadiths indicates that they could not both have belonged to the same person. It is as we have said: The Qur'an, which has no similar or parallel in the language, is the product of the One who Himself has nothing bearing any similarity to any of His attributes, the Almighty who hears all and sees all.

Chapter 7

The Secret of the Qur'anic Miracle

> Let us now assume that a person who seeks the truth has followed our line of argument and conducted his own research, looking into all the evidence, making comparisons of style and language, distinguishing fine and superb styles from what is inferior to them, yet still he remains in doubt. Such a person would now say to us: I have indeed looked at all the different styles of expression and examined them all very carefully. I admit that there is nothing as powerful or as fine and enchanting as the Qur'an. I accept that it is, as you describe it, absolutely unique, surpassing, overpowering and that nothing stands up to it. Nevertheless, I feel something within me that I cannot explain, making me eager to study the special characteristics and features that distinguish the Qur'an from all other speech. For these form the secret of its miraculous nature. Would you explain some of these to me for reassurance.

Such a request is by no means easy. It is a goal that has preoccupied scholars and men of letters of past and present generations. Yet they have not achieved their whole purpose. All that they could do is to give examples and analogies. They have admitted that what remained hidden, after all their efforts, is greater than what they have fathomed. They also say that what they describe of the portions they have learnt is less than what they felt to be indescribable.

The Secret of the Qur'anic Miracle

Now that the task has fallen to us, we cannot do better than to follow in their footsteps. We certainly cannot outline the whole secret that makes the Qur'an so miraculous, nor can we present all miraculous aspects people have defined, nor all that we ourselves feel of these aspects. We will only attempt to describe some aspects that we feel whenever we listen to the Qur'an, or read parts of it, or when we reflect on the meaning of its verses. You may find in a few of these what you will not find in many aspects outlined by other people. Nonetheless, we hope that our discussion will be of benefit to you and will give you firmer conviction.

The first thing that attracts attention in the Qur'anic style is its sound structure in form and substance. Let a fine reciter of the Qur'an begin his recitation, with proper care, letting himself follow the drift of the passage he is reading, not making it follow his own preferences. Now move away from him and sit in a place where you cannot distinguish the sounds of the different letters, but rather you will be able to hear the general sound, with its vowels and their elongation, nasalised consonants, sequences of sounds and stops. Listen very carefully to this cluster of sounds as they are left idle, unidentifiable as letters and words. You will find in them a remarkable tune that you can never find in any other speech you hear in the same way, superbly recited as it may be.

What you find in these unidentifiable sounds of a Qur'anic recitation is coherence akin to that of music and poetry, but it reflects neither musical tunes nor poetic metre. But you will also find something that is found neither in music nor in poetry. When we listen to a poem we find that it follows the same metre, line after line. Similarly, a musical tune must have a uniting rhythm. Hence, we get tired of it when it is repeated time after time. In the case of the Qur'an, you have a varied and ever renewing tune which moves between single or clusters of consonants, followed by short and long vowels, and culminating with the ending of verses. These follow a wide range of patterns, each of which is so appealing that you do not feel any boredom when it is recited time after time. You will always ask for more.

Such rhythmic excellence in the Qur'anic language is appreciated by everyone who listens to the Qur'an when it is being recited, even though such a person may not speak Arabic. How, then, can it go unnoticed by the Arabs?

Some people may wonder why, in their disputes about the Qur'an, the Arabs compared it to poetry in order to prove their point or to disprove the opposing point. Why have they not compared it to any other form of address, including public speech? Can we identify here the secret the Arabs felt, but which has remained overlooked by those for whom Arabic is not their native language?

The first thing the refined Arabian ear felt in the composition of the Qur'an was that remarkable sound order which arranges consonants and short and long vowels in varied patterns that keeps listeners alert. Longer vowels and nasalised sounds are interspersed in between in a most appropriate proportion that ensures refined tuning and easy flow until the ending of a verse is reached. The Arabs of old attempted something of this nature in their poetry, but they carried it to extremes, furnishing in the reader or listener boredom caused by endless repetition. But the Arabs never used such refinements in prose, whether it was left free or maintained a rhyme. Indeed, the reverse is true. In prose, we always find defects that detract from the easy flow of speech. Such defects make it impossible to recite prose without adding something here or deleting something there.

It is no wonder, then, that the nearest classification of the Qur'an in the Arab's imagination was to say that it was poetry. They found in its rhythm something that can only be found in poetry. Yet when they reflected upon it a little, they readily admitted that it was not poetry. As al-Walīd ibn al-Mughīrah stated: It is unlike all forms and styles of poetry. Again it is no wonder that when they were at a loss how to describe it, they called it a type of sorcery, because it achieves a happy medium between what is free and what is constrained. It reflects the power of prose together with the beauty and refinement of poetry.

The Secret of the Qur'anic Miracle

Now if you draw nearer to the reciter so as to hear each sound accurately realised at its proper place of articulation, you will be surprised at how these sounds are superbly arranged. Voiced, voiceless, fricative and plosive sounds flow in an easy and powerful arrangement presenting a language so superb and beautiful it leaves no room for any defect in the line of speech. The Qur'anic style follows neither the soft urban pattern, nor the rough bedouin one. Indeed, it combines the power of the desert people's language with the refinement and easy flow of urban speech, without allowing either pattern to dominate. Thus, it gives us a perfect mix, as though it includes the best characteristics of both types of language. It may be described as the meeting point of all Arabian tribes. It is appreciated and admired by all.

The Inimitability of the Qur'anic Style

In fact these two aspects form the outer surface of the beauty of the Qur'an, but this covering is similar to a beautiful shell hiding a superb and precious pearl. It is part of the laws God Almighty has set for this world that He would cover great secrets with a screen that reflects beauty and brings enjoyment. This helps to preserve them and heighten competition to learn and treasure them. Consider how He made the desire for food and the bond of love a means to ensure the survival of the individual and the human community. Similarly, as He has willed to protect the treasured wealth of knowledge He has included in the Qur'an, He, in His wisdom, has determined to give it a superb framework which endears it to people and enhances their eagerness to grasp it. It serves as a motive which urges them to work for it and makes their effort easier to exert. He has undoubtedly selected a superb pattern of the Arabic language. This ensures that the voice of the Qur'an will continue to be heard by people as long as they have tongues to articulate it and ears to listen to it, even though most of them continue to fall short of appreciating its inner meaning and are unable to recognise its message. *"It is We Ourselves who have bestowed this reminder from on high, and it is We who shall truly preserve it."* (15: 9.)

Are you now fully aware that the construction of the Qur'an combines with its beauty an element of power and peculiarity? And do you know that this beauty of the Qur'an has served as additional strength, which God has granted, to protect the Qur'an and preserve it intact?

In fact, this peculiarity has served as an element adding more power to the argument of the Qur'an as it challenged people to produce something similar to it. It has given the Qur'an protection against those who would imitate it or alter its arrangement. Its beauty would not have been sufficient, on its own, to deter them. In fact, it would have tempted them to do just that. The point is that when people admire something, they try to imitate it and compete in following its pattern. We have seen how literary figures follow one another in their fine styles. A man of letters living in a later age may achieve the same or a higher standard than an earlier figure he admires. This is the case among writers and public speakers. Indeed, all styles in prose and poetry follow trodden paths. These they learn, and in imitating them they train, just as one would do in any trade or skill.

What, then, has stopped people from attacking the Qur'an with their tongues and pens, when they have always admired its style, especially when so many of them would have loved to meet its challenge and refute its argument?

The reason is that the Qur'an has a natural immunity which restrains all people from imitating it. The first element in this immunity is that which we have already described of its unique arrangement of sounds, and its remarkable construction starting with letters and words and extending to phrases, sentences and verses. These are arranged in a particular thread, giving the Qur'an its unique character that is unlike any style people have ever used or are likely to use. Hence, they have not found a pattern to follow in order to imitate the Qur'an. Essentially, it is impossible to follow its pattern. Proof of this rests in the fact that if anyone tries to introduce into it anything that people have composed, in times gone by, or now or in the future, be it the work of men of letters, earlier prophets or anyone whomsoever, its mode

The Secret of the Qur'anic Miracle

will be distorted to all readers. Its rhythm will jar in every ear. The phrases so introduced will stand out as alien to it. The Qur'an will not assimilate any of it. *"It is a sublime, Divine book. No falsehood can ever attain to it, neither openly nor in a stealthy manner. It is bestowed from on high by One who is truly wise, ever to be praised."* (41: 41-42.)

If you are not distracted by the outer beauty and the fine coverings, and you continue to pursue the secret inside, trying to open the shell in order to find the treasured pearl, you have to move from the vocal pattern to the order of meanings. There you will find what is vastly superior and far more appealing.

We will not talk here about what the Qur'an includes of scientific fact that remains beyond the attainment of ordinary mortals. This is a subject which we will tackle when we speak about the scientific challenge of the Qur'an. For now we are concentrating on the linguistic challenge, and here we are only concerned with words and sentences.

Words are sometimes considered from the point of view of their being an utterance composed of sound clusters indicating vowels and consonants, without looking at their meaning. We have already discussed this aspect. Alternatively, words are considered from the point of view of their meanings which the speaker wants to convey to those whom he addresses. This is the aspect we will be tackling presently. This is undoubtedly the aspect that reflects far more clearly the linguistic challenge that we are considering. Language is all about the expression of meaning, and it is in this respect that styles are evaluated, rather than in their rhythm and music.

As for the meaning of the Qur'an from the point of view of the wealth of scientific knowledge it includes, this is a different area altogether. It goes beyond any linguistic study. Literary excellence relies on the accuracy of the images portrayed and the fine expressions conveying the intended meaning. It is immaterial in this respect whether the meaning concerns the nature of human thoughts or something that goes beyond this, a practical fact or an allegory, a true fact or a falsehood. In fact, the Qur'anic expression of what the non-believers said is as superb in style as the rest of the Qur'an, because it describes their thoughts most perfectly. Scientific excellence, on the other hand, relies on the meaning itself, regardless of the way it is expressed. It is true that linguistic styles may differ in expressing the meaning fully, which means that an excellent expression of a scientific idea may add to its value, but then we are speaking about the mode of expression, not the subject to be expressed. Let us, then, leave this scientific point for now in order to concentrate on the linguistic one.

We will begin now to describe some aspects of the Qur'anic method of expression, tackling these in four different categories: 1) a passage; 2) a surah; 3) a group of surahs; and 4) the Qur'an as a whole.

Perhaps we should explain here that when we speak of a passage we are talking about a portion that conveys a complete meaning like what is conveyed in several verses or a long verse. This is the minimum the challenge thrown down in the Qur'an for imitation requires. It asks the doubters to produce 'a single surah like it', not a long or a medium length surah. This general statement includes the short surahs, most of which were revealed in Makkah, including the shortest ones.

Some people have suggested that the challenge does not refer to any surah, but to one 'in which the quality of literary style is clearly seen.' This suggests that such quality does not appear fully in three verses or so. This does not detract from the superiority of the Qur'an. Yet whoever said this has based it on his own thought to which he has no proof. He simply excluded the short surahs from being miraculous in nature. He has seen no peculiarity in their style, and as such could not see how the challenge applies to them as well. But this is evidence of his own inability. Such a person should have reflected on the fact that the Arabs at the time of the Prophet could not produce anything like the short or long surahs of the Qur'an. In their view, all were infinitely superior to their own talents. This is sufficient evidence if he wishes, but he could also try to assimilate the meaning of a short surah and express this meaning in words of his own choosing. He will inevitably find that he has only two alternatives: either he will not be able to express its meaning in a similarly effective style and appropriate arrangement, or he will have to use exactly the same words as the Qur'an has used, and in the same order. This exercise will show him that the secret of the superior excellence of the Qur'an is apparent in its longer surahs as in the shorter ones. It is just like the secret of creation being evident in an ant as it is evident in an elephant. Ibn ᶜAṭiyyah says: "We appreciate the excellence in most of the Qur'an, but we are unaware of it in some places, because our linguistic taste falls short of that of the Arabs at the time. The argument has been proven for all mankind when the Arabs of the time demonstrated their inability to produce anything like the Qur'an. They were the most eloquent of all people."

Chapter 8

Surpassing Excellence in Every Passage

It is very difficult to try to describe the style of the Qur'an which defies imitation. It is perhaps sufficient to say that it combines every good quality in literary style, even though such qualities may move in opposite directions. This needs a full explanation, which is easily felt but more difficult to express. We will, however, try to give a partial explanation as best we can. But before we do that, we will outline some aspects of human speech which are easily understood by everyone who attempts literary expression. This will enable us to contrast the shortcomings of human style with the perfection of the Qur'an.

Concise but fully expressive

These are two widely different aims. Whoever tries to combine both of them together finds himself like one caught between two women: he cannot maintain justice between them, without finding himself constantly leaning towards one or the other. When he tries to economise with words, using only what is adequate, he must inevitably lose part of the meaning. He may try to express his meaning in general terms. If he is making an argument, he may say, "Believe this, or do not believe that." In description, he would confine himself to saying, "This is beautiful, and that is ugly." If he is making a report, he would say, "This has taken place, and that did not." When he makes a request, he says, "Do this, and do not do that." Alternatively, he may add some details, but will continue to be very cautious of saying more than he needs. Thus, he leaves out whatever he can, dispensing with preliminaries

Surpassing Excellence in Every Passage

and omitting those tools which raise expectation, adding emphasis, generating interest and similarly essential elements of fine speech. Thus, what he comes up with is akin to a garment that is too short or too tight, or like a skeleton that has not been fleshed up. Sometimes the omission of a particle will considerably reduce the beauty of a sentence, leaving it too dry or too dull. It is often the case that an attempt to shorten a piece of writing will leave it too vague to understand.

On the other hand, a person who tries to express his meaning fully, doing justice to its finer details, as far as he understands or feels it, must allow himself sufficient space. He will not find economy of words serving his purpose. He feels the need to explain his thoughts fully. When he tries this, he will inevitably use an expansive style. He may take his time before he arrives at the conclusion he wants to make. You may begin to lose interest before you complete reading.

Most men and women of letters, of old and modern times, often err on the side of saying more than they need in order to express their meaning. They rarely choose to be too concise. Indeed, most of them find it tempting to display their literary ability. Some resort to using unfamiliar words and constructions, forcing the reader to read a sentence more than once in order to gather its meaning. Thus, the extra words or expressions used make the meaning less clear. Others use too many words, thus making their style verbose, longwinded or effusive. Or they make their reader stumble in his attempt to grasp the meaning because they use too many synonyms or analogous words. They think that by so doing, they make their meaning succinct, while in fact they make it too thin. Perhaps the best among these is one whose writings could be reduced by half without losing anything of what he wishes to express.

Hard as they try, people of fine literary talent rarely, if ever, achieve their target. The maximum they can achieve is a relative perfection, 'in as much as they can fathom or reflect a moment of inspiration.' To express a certain idea fully and perfectly, without falling short in one or more aspects of it, or adding something that does not really belong to it, allowing no room for suggesting anything new, is something no one who has attempted fine literary expression will ever claim for himself, let alone for others. If he were to review what he has written, time after time, he would inevitably find something to modify, or an omission to be redressed, or some thought to be brought forward or taken backward, in order to make it flow better. If he were to review it 70 times, as the pre-Islamic Arab poet, Zuhayr ibn Abi Sulma, used to review his poems which he called, 'the annuals', he would have something to change every time. The more refined he is, the less satisfied with his product he will be. He will always feel that he is short of the ideal to which he aspires. He is like the one described in a Qur'anic analogy, '*stretching out his hand to the water in the hope that it will reach his mouth, but it will never reach it.*' (13: 24.)

This is what he may feel about his own product. But what will his critics and competitors say? We should remember here that in all this he is striving to achieve one aim. What will be the result if he tries to achieve the other end at the same time, putting his wealth of meaning in the most concise of forms? How can he achieve both ends when he is a prisoner of his human nature that cannot get nearer to one end of the road unless it goes further away from the other?

If we find that someone has managed to achieve both ends in one or two sentences, we need to consider carefully what he says thereafter. For it is inevitable that he will soon tire himself out. His powerful style will give way, and his bright style will soon lose its shine. He will achieve that great height only occasionally, just like we find a piece of precious metal in a great heap of rock. When you consider what such a writer has written you will say to different parts of it, "This is good; and this is superior; but that is the finest piece."

Let us ask any literary critic of recognised high standing: "Have you ever come across a poem or a piece of literary prose with clear meaning, concise expression and fine construction throughout?" We will find them all

Surpassing Excellence in Every Passage

unanimous that even the finest of poets achieve real excellence in only a few lines within a few poems. Beyond that, they may have what is average, run of the mill or even of lower standard. They would say the same about orators and writers. Indeed, such shortcomings are clearer in their case.

If you wish to see how these two qualities of precision and concise construction, go hand in hand in perfect measure, throughout a piece of work, you only need to look anywhere you wish in the Qur'an. You are bound to find literary expression that fits the purpose perfectly, without leaning towards expansion or inadequacy. Every idea and every point is given in a clear and full picture. It is clear in the sense that it has no trace of anything alien to it. It is also full, omitting nothing of its essential elements or complementary requisites. Yet at the same time, it is expressed in the finest and most concise style. Every word, particle or letter has a purpose to serve. The place of every word in every sentence, and the position of every sentence in a verse are carefully selected so as to produce the finest meaning, flowing from one idea to the next.

Put your hand over any page of the Qur'an you choose, and count the number of words you have covered. Then select an equal number of the most expressive words in human speech other than those in the Qur'an and compare the meaning in both cases. [Although the Prophet's own style is the most concise and eloquent human speech, it is far less concise and rich in meaning than the Qur'an.] Consider then how many words you may delete or replace in this second passage without loss of meaning, and consider if you can do the same with the Qur'an. The fact is, as stated by Ibn ʿAṭiyyah, a famous Arab literary critic, that if we were to screen the whole Arabic language in search of a word to replace one word of the Qur'an expressing the meaning equally, let alone more fully, we will find none. It is aptly described by God Himself: *"This is a Scripture with verses which have been set out with perfection and then expounded in detail, bestowed on you by Him who is Wise, All-Aware."* (11: 1.)

Let us now examine this verse very carefully. The whole idea we have discussed is combined here in two phrases, each expressed in a single Arabic word in the original text: "set out with perfection", and "expounded". This is a most apt description of the Qur'anic style. It is perfected by the One who is 'Wise' and who leaves no defect in what He produces. It is also expounded by the same One who is 'All-Aware', and who knows every detail of every living thing.

Addressing the general public or select groups

These are two widely differing aims. If you were to speak to highly intelligent people in a simple style, explaining every little and simple detail, as you need to do when addressing people of average intelligence, you will offend them, as they will consider this approach to be beneath them. On the other hand, if you were to address the general public in a concise manner, making only a hint here and a brief reference there, as you should do when you speak to educated and intelligent people, you will heavily tax their mental faculties. Hence, if you want your meaning to be equally understood by both groups, you have to address them separately, using different styles and approaches. The matter is the same as when addressing children and adults. No single style is good for both.

To address highly educated, intelligent people in the top echelon of society with the same words addressed to people who are uneducated, of limited intelligence and occupying a lower position on the social ladder, and to fully satisfy them all is something beyond human ability. Indeed, it is not found anywhere other than in the Qur'an. It is the same book found most satisfying by those who appreciate literary refinements. At the same time, ordinary people find it easy to grasp, free of ambiguity or confusion. It gives pleasure to both groups, placing no burden on either. *"Indeed, We made this Qur'an easy to bear in mind: who, then, is willing to take it to heart?"* (54: 17.)

Surpassing Excellence in Every Passage

Logical conviction and emotional satisfaction

Two forces are always active within a human being: the intellectual and the emotional. They have different roles and directions. The first aims to know the truth, and to identify what is good and beneficial so as to adopt it. The other records its feelings of pain and pleasure. A perfect style is that which satisfies both needs at the same time, giving you intellectual satisfaction and emotional pleasure, like a bird flying with two wings.

Do we find such perfection in human style? We have seen the writings of scientists and philosophers, and works of poets and fine prose and fiction writers, but we find it all tilting to one side or the other. The former present to us their thoughts in a direct manner, addressing our intellect with the facts, without in any way trying to appeal to our emotions. Thus, when they present scientific facts, they do not care that they may sound dull and uninteresting. Poets, on the other hand, try to appeal to our feelings and emotions. They do not care whether what they present is fact or fancy, real or imaginary. They sound serious when they are jesting, inviting tears without weeping themselves, enchanting their audience without being enchanted. *"Poets are followed only by those who are lost in grievous error. Do you not see that they roam confusedly through all the valleys [of words and thoughts], and that they say what they do not do? Except for those who believe and do good deeds, and remember God often, and defend themselves after having been wronged."* (26: 224-7.)

Everyone is a kind of a philosopher when he thinks, and a kind of a poet when he feels. Ask, if you will, psychologists and psychiatrists if they have ever seen anyone in whom their intellectual power is of the same strength as their emotional one, and as all other psychological forces. If these powers are somehow of comparable strength among a small number of people, do they influence a person in the same way at the same time? They will all answer you that this does not happen at all. These forces will only act one at a time. Whenever any one of them is dominant, the others dwindle into the background, making practically no influence on what is taking place. When a person is deeply involved in his intellectual thoughts, he does not give much way to his feelings and emotions. A person enjoying some pleasurable experience, or enduring pain, will not have much time for intellectual thought. The fact is that human beings do not pursue these two aims simultaneously. Otherwise, they would be going forward and backward at the same time, and this is not possible. It is just like God says: *"Never has God endowed any man with two hearts in one body."* (33: 4) How can we, then, expect a human being to address both pursuits with the same vigour when they do not co-exist within him with the same strength at any one time? Indeed, whatever we say reflects our mood at the time of speaking.

In fact this is a standard that gives us an idea of the force a writer or a speaker was under at the time of writing or speaking. If he tries to establish a theoretical premise or a practical method, we conclude that his writing reflects an intellectual mood. If, on the other hand, he tries to excite feelings, playing on emotions of pleasure and grief, happiness and sadness, we determine that his work reflects an emotional mood. If he moves from one aspect to the other, giving each one his total concentration, we realise that logical thinking is alternating with emotional feeling within him. For the same style to maintain both aspects at the same time, like one branch of a tree carries leaves, flowers and fruits all together, or like the spirit permeates the body, or water goes through a green plant, is unknown in human speech. Indeed, it is incompatible with human nature.

Who, then, can come up with a discourse that presents hard facts in an argument which is well accepted by the most intellectual of philosophers, and combines it with emotional pleasure that satisfies carefree poets? This is something that can only be achieved by God, the Lord of all worlds. He is the One who is never preoccupied with something to the exclusion of another. He is the One able to address the intellect and the emotion at the same time, and to mix beauty with the truth in a way that neither trespasses over the other. These ingredients make up a uniquely exotic and most enjoyable drink. This is what we all find in His glorious Book, whatever part we read. Read, if you will, Surah 12, which is devoted entirely to the story of Joseph,

Surpassing Excellence in Every Passage

or Surah 28, which devotes more than half its verses to the story of Moses. In both, you find that relating at leisure the details of the story does not lead to any missing out on the moral of the event or a blurring of the lessons to be drawn from the story.

Even in the midst of providing intellectual proof, or outlining legal provisions, the emotional aspect is not overlooked. We have even in these instances what arouses our interest, heightens our feelings, or even a warning, or a statement of amazement or reproach, etc. All these are provided at the beginning or the end of its verses, or within them. Hence, the Qur'an is aptly described as the Book that: *"makes the skins of those who stand in awe of their Lord shiver; but in the end, their skins and hearts soften with the remembrance of God."* (39: 23.) *"This is surely a decisive word; it is no frivolity."* (86: 13-14.)

Let us now take two examples in support of what we have just said. The first is one that mixes logical proof with emotional address. Verse 22 of *Surah* 21 may be given in translation as follows: *"Had there been in heaven or on earth any deities other than God, both would surely have fallen into ruin! Exalted is God, Lord of the Throne, above what they describe."* Consider how these few words provide logical proof and excite amazement at the enormity of what is alleged. In fact, the evidence given brings together undoubted and fully accepted premises with a vivid description of the ruin that results from an inevitable conflict. Thus, the evidence is given in a poetic style. Do we ever find anything like this in a book of theoretical wisdom?

The second example is a text outlining legal provisions: *"Believers, just retribution is ordained for you in cases of killing: the free for the free, and the slave for the slave, and the woman for the woman. And if something [of his guilt] is remitted to a guilty person by his brother, this [remission] shall be adhered to in fairness, and restitution to his fellow-man shall be made in goodly manner. This is an alleviation from your Lord, and an act of His grace. And for him who, none the less, wilfully transgresses the bounds of what is right, there is grievous suffering in store."* (2: 178.) Consider how the verse opens with emphasis on obedience reflected in making the address to 'believers'. The element of grievance is then reduced between the families of the killer and the victim by using such words as, *'his brother'*, *'in fairness'*, and *'in goodly manner.'* Then there is a reminder of God's favours in the statement, *'This is an alleviation from your Lord, and an act of His grace,'* which is then followed by a warning at the end of the verse. Now consider the subject matter of this verse. It is speaking about duties in a case of killing. The same applies to all verses outlining legal provisions, including those speaking of strained marital relationships, divorce and other methods of separation. In what book of law do we find such a spirit? In what language do we find such a mixture? If anyone tries to make such combination, exerting every effort and straining himself as much as he can, all that he will come up with is a host of contradictions making his writing look like a garment that has been patched up after extensive tears.

General and clear

This is a unique combination that we do not find anywhere other than in the Qur'an. The thing is that when people make their thoughts well defined, they do not leave room for any interpretation. If they make it general, they make their style ambiguous or even confusing, or they leave it totally unclear. It is practically impossible to combine these two aims of clarity and generality.

When you read a passage of the Qur'an, however, you find it transparently clear, with precision in expressing the intended meaning, and without any alien word or concept to confuse the issue in question. It requires no hard thinking or repetition of the statement; its meaning is readily apparent. You feel as though you are not listening to words and statements, but looking at images and well established facts. You tend to think that you have gathered its meaning in full. Yet if you were to read it again at a later time, you will find that you see in it a new meaning that differs from the one you had gathered the first time. The same may happen time and again, so that the same

Surpassing Excellence in Every Passage

sentence, or the same word, may have several correct, or potentially correct, interpretations. It is comparable to a diamond, each side of which gives a different ray. If you were to take a total view of it, you have an amazing spectrum, comprising the whole colours of a rainbow. You feel unable to decide what to take and what to leave out. If you were to let another person look at it, he may see in it more than you do.

We will give here a small example. Take the Qur'anic statement: *"God grants sustenance without reckoning, to whom He wills."* (2: 212.) This is certainly very clear to all minds. Yet at the same time, there is a great deal of flexibility. If you were to say that it means that God gives sustenance to His servants without accounting to anyone about what He does, and without anyone asking Him why has He given some people in abundance and given others limited means, you are correct. If you say that it means that when He gives, He does not reckon up what He has given for fear that resources may be exhausted, you are correct. If you take it to mean that He gives people their sustenance from where they cannot reckon, you are correct. Similarly, you are correct to say that He gives His servants their sustenance without putting them first to account for their deeds. If you finally say that it means that He gives sustenance in abundance, without measure and subject to no calculation, you are correct.

In the first meaning, the statement provides a rule for the granting of God's provisions. The system does not operate on the basis of what the recipient deserves according to his knowledge or deeds. Provisions are determined by God's will, as He wishes to test His servants. This provides consolation to the poor among the believers and puts the rich and arrogant face to face with the facts so that they do not go too far in their conceit. The second meaning alerts us to the limitless resources God has at His command, and that He gives in abundance as He wills. The third meaning provides a hint to the believers of what God will give them of victories so as to replace their hard times with comfort and their poverty with affluence. All this will come about from where they do not reckon. The last two meanings give a promise to the good believers either to be admitted to heaven without having to face the reckoning, or to multiply their reward manifold. Whoever looks at how scholars interpret Qur'anic verses will be amazed at what they come up with.

Thus, we see a book laid open at all times. Everyone takes from it what they are able to take, as fits their different talents and purposes. We see indeed an endless ocean stretching beyond imagination. It has accommodated all schools of thought, different as their methodologies and rules of deduction are. It has also catered for all scientific theories, ancient and modern, different as their methods and means are. Easy to understand and analyse as it is, it retains its vigour and power, remaining free of change and contradiction. Each party finds in it a basis for its argument, claiming its support. Yet, in its sublimity, it remains above them all, looking from on high to see them fighting over it as though he is telling them: *"Say, Everyone acts according to his own disposition. Your Lord is fully aware who is best guided."* (17: 84.)

One Example of the Qur'anic Style

We have so far explained some of the characteristics that make the Qur'anic style unique, not only in the Arabic language, but in human speech generally. We have showed how it combines characteristics that are not found together in any other style. We gave examples in each case. Now we will give another example, drawing the reader's attention particularly to the precision of expression and powerful construction in the Qur'anic style. It uses both qualities in order to provide rich meaning in the most concise form. This particular quality is the one most in need of explanation.

But we will not take, for our example, any of the verses that have been admiringly discussed by literary figures over the centuries, such as the verse which says: *"There is life for you, men of understanding, in this code of just retribution."* (2: 179.) Nor shall we take the highly descriptive, yet particularly concise verse which describes the end of the great floods at the time of Noah: *"And the word was spoken: You earth, swallow up your waters; and you sky, cease [your rain]! And the waters sank into the earth, and the will of God was done, and the ark came to rest on Mount Judi. And the word was spoken:*

Surpassing Excellence in Every Passage

'Away with these evildoing folk!'" (11: 44.) We will not take these, nor indeed any similar example. We will take, instead, a passage speaking of something that people hardly ever associate with literary excellence. This will give us a fair idea of what we mean when we speak about the inimitability of the Qur'anic style.

Speaking about the arguments the Jews in Madinah advanced in their rejection of the message of Islam, God says: *"When they are told: 'Believe in what God has revealed,' they say: 'We believe in what has been revealed to us.' But they deny the truth of everything beyond that, although it be the truth corroborating that which they have. Say: 'Why, then, did you of old kill the prophets sent by God, if you are true believers?' Moses came to you with clear signs but, in his absence, you worshipped the calf and thus became transgressors. We accepted your solemn pledge and raised Mount Sinai above you [and said], 'Take with firmness and strength what We have given you, and hearken to it.' They said: 'We hear but we disobey.' They were made to drink the calf into their very hearts because of their disbelief. Say: 'Vile is that which your faith enjoins upon you, if indeed you are believers.'"* (2: 91-3.)

These verses form only a passage in one chapter of the story of the Children of Israel. The main elements that stand out in this short passage may be summed up as follows:

- An advice to the Jews, calling on them to accept the Qur'an as God's revelation;
- Their reply to this advice, which has a dual purpose;
- A refutation of this reply in both its purposes, using several arguments in this refutation.

If a lawyer of exceptional ability was given the task of defending the Qur'an in this particular issue, and he was able to organise his thoughts around these points, I swear he would not express them as fully as the Qur'an even though he may use several times the number of words used in these verses. Even then he will not be able to include the finer elements we find in the Qur'anic statement.

The advice to the Jews says to them: Believe in the Qur'an like you believed in the Torah. Since your belief in the latter is based on the fact that God revealed it to Moses, the Qur'an preached by Muhammad is also revealed by God. Hence, you should believe in the latter as you believed in the former.

This is the gist of the advice, but all this is expressed in the Qur'an in a most economic statement: *"Believe in what God has revealed."* It does not mention the Qur'an by name, but by a clear reference to it. This gives the advantage of giving the argument for this advice in the very words it is made. Moreover, it does not mention by name the Prophet to whom the Qur'an is revealed, although mentioning it would have provided a fuller description of the Qur'an in which they are required to believe. This is because mentioning it makes no special addition to the point being expressed, and because it is counterproductive in as far as the effect of the advice is concerned. From a literary point of view, mentioning the name of the Prophet Muhammad in this advice does not add anything special to their duty to believe in the Qur'an. Hence, the advice is based on the common grounds on which the argument for such belief relies. On the other hand, mentioning the name of Muhammad may alert the grudges of those who are hostile to him. Thus, it may undermine the purpose of bringing peace and unity which the advice aims to achieve.

Moreover, the omission of the Prophet's name is more in line with Islam, which is a religion aiming to unite people after they have been divided by their divergent beliefs. It calls on people to believe in all God's revelations to Abraham, Ishmael, Isaac, Jacob and the tribes, and also in what was revealed to Moses and Jesus and other prophets. We do not make any distinction between God's revelations, just as we do not make any distinction between His Messengers.

Surpassing Excellence in Every Passage

The Jews' reply confirms that they believed in the Torah not only because it was revealed by God, but because He revealed it to them. As the Qur'an was not similarly revealed to them, they would have nothing to do with it. They continue to believe only in their Torah. Let each nation have its own faith. All this is summed up in the Qur'anic statement quoting their reply: "*We believe in what has been revealed to us.*" This is the first purpose in their reply. The statement is further reduced by deleting the name of the One who sends revelations, i.e. God, because He is mentioned in the previous statement: "*Believe in what God has revealed.*"

It is clear that restricting themselves to believing in only what is revealed to them means that they deny what is revealed to anyone else. This is the second purpose, but they try to keep it implicit in order not to admit their disbelief. But the Qur'an highlights this, although it does not make it a logical conclusion of their belief. It does not add to their statement what it implies. It simply states it by way of explaining what they actually said: "*But they deny the truth of everything beyond that.*" Thus, we see an example of the strictest honesty in reporting.

Now reflect for a moment on the use of the phrase, '*everything beyond that.*' This may be understood in two ways: the first includes everything in addition to the Qur'an, and the second is more restricted. The fact is that they did not only deny the Qur'an revealed to Muhammad, but they also denied the Gospel revealed to Jesus. Both were revealed '*beyond*', or after, the Torah. They did not deny what was revealed before the Torah, such as Abraham's scrolls. Their crime is, thus, defined so precisely by using this term, most truthful and most fair as it is.

Decisive Refutation of Counter Arguments

Having stated the case, the passage now refutes their arguments, both explicit and implicit. It begins by leaving aside their claim of believing in their revealed book, as though it is a proven fact, so that it takes it as a basis for the requirement to believe in other revealed books. It asks: How can it be that their belief in the book revealed to them a reason for disbelieving in what is similarly true, or indeed in what is 'the truth'? Does the new revelation run contrary to the truth so that believing in one book necessitates disbelieving in the other? The argument is then taken a step further showing that different things may be equally true but have no bearing, one on the other, as they are unrelated. But this new revelation is a witness for earlier ones, confirming their truth. How can it, then, be rejected by those who believe in such earlier revelations?

The line of argument is thus taken to its logical conclusion. It points out that if the distortion that had found its way into those earlier books obliterated all aspects of the truth in them, they might have some justification in rejecting the Qur'an. It might have been possible for them to argue that what remains of their books does not have an identical import with that of the Qur'an. Hence, believing in them does not necessarily require believing in it. Indeed they would have been similarly justified in their rejection if that remaining portion of the truth in their book was not available to them. But the Qur'an confirmed and corroborated the truth that remained with them and was being studied by them. How, then, can they justify their rejection? The whole of this point is expressed in the Qur'anic text by the phrase, *'although it is the truth corroborating that which they have'*.

We note that the logical usage here should have included different words, such as, 'corroborating that which was revealed to them,' but the Qur'an gives a different heading to their book, with special significance and suitability to the present context. Had the Qur'anic statement said, for example, 'corroborating that which remains with them now', the expression would have lost the element of commitment binding on them to believe in the Qur'an. Here, we are discussing a change that would affect only a couple of words, but even then, it would be decisive in the refutation of all their argument. As it is, the Qur'anic expression is made in a very short phrase, but it nevertheless leaves them no way out. If we were to compare this to military action, we may say that it is one step taken swiftly, without any noise, to place the opposition under complete siege.

Surpassing Excellence in Every Passage

Having treated this implied aspect which the Qur'an presents as an objection, the passage undertakes to refute their main, declared objection given in their boastful statement that they believe in only what is revealed to them. It shows that it is a false argument. Indeed, their rejection of the truth is a chronic illness they have had for centuries. Their rejection of what is revealed to Muhammad is merely one link in the long chain of their disbelief, even in what was revealed to them. Evidence in plenty is given to confirm this: their ignorance of God, ill-treatment of His Messengers, and disobedience of His orders: "*Say: Why, then, did you of old kill the prophets sent by God, if you are true believers?*"

1. Reflect first how the switch of subject is well prepared. The audience understand from the rejection by the Jews of what corroborates their book that they, in fact, deny their own book as well. Can a person who rejects an argument in your favour be your best advocate? But this point is deduced from what they say, committing them to what their boasting entails. It is not taken directly from their attitude. That is left to what now follows. We see, then, how the phrase, '*although it be the truth corroborating that which they have*,' serves as a close of one aspect and an opening of another. It is like the last step in the first flight of stairs being the first in the next flight. This makes the whole passage very closely knit together. In fact, the literary expression is made to suit the feelings of the listener most perfectly, as and when these feelings develop. When the listener, having heard this word, is felt to look for a conclusion, the conclusion is provided in all clarity.

2. In fact the Qur'an does not mention the real perpetrators of those crimes. It does not say to them, 'Why did your forefathers kill God's Messengers, or why did they worship the calf, or why did they say: We hear and we disobey.' That would be a false argument in the first place, similar to the argument of the wolf which justified his intended eating of the lamb by saying that the lamb's father disturbed the stream a year earlier causing him to drink muddy water. Had this been used as an argument, they would be justified in saying in reply: "Our forefathers

are long gone, and no one should be held responsible for the misdeeds of another." Had that argument been used and supported by saying that the present generation takes the same stand as the old one, it would still be a hollow argument. Hence, the whole argument has been summed up, making the indictment applicable to them directly, showing that they are in the same position as their forefathers. The crime is equally theirs. Whichever of them you accuse, you will easily prove your case. They simply follow in their forefathers footsteps, pursuing the same objectives.

3. This concept is further enhanced by the usage of the present tense in describing the first crime of murdering prophets, as though it took place at the same time as the Qur'an was revealed. It is as though these same people are caught red-handed.

4. Such usage of the present tense, and mentioning God's prophets collectively, could have generated a feeling of grief in Prophet Muhammad's heart, and might have tempted his enemies into thinking that their schemes to kill him might yet succeed. Hence, all this is forestalled by use of the phrase, *'of old'*, to make them despair of any success in their present schemes. It gives the Prophet reassurance, as though it is a full promise that they will not harm him. The phrase also serves as a reminder that all this took place in the past, but the use of the present tense in Arabic is intentional.

5. It is to be noted that as the passage lists their other offences, it uses the past tense, having prepared our minds for this change with the addition of the phrase, *'of old'*, so that the historical perspective is made clear.

6. The next offence mentioned is far worse than the first, because it means the association of partners with God. But the Qur'anic reference to it is so refined that it deletes the second object. It does not say to them, 'you have made the calf a deity to worship'. The deletion adds a sense of strong abhorrence to their deed.

7. There are several instances where details are left out. This is because these details are not particularly essential. The Qur'an is stated clearly to corroborate what they have, but we have no information to tell us how far the corroboration extends, and whether it relates only to the fundamentals of faith or to its details as well, and which details, if any. This because kings speak only in measured speech. Why should the one who calls on people to believe be concerned with how far two religions agree on something or another? This is left to jurists. The passage states that they killed prophets, without specifying the names of the prophets they killed. This is left to historians. It states that Moses brought them clear proofs, but does not specify what these were. Nor does it mention the nature of the solemn pledges he accepted from them. None of these details is of importance at this specific juncture. Had they been mentioned, it would be like the person who has just beaten his servant answering a question on the reason for so doing. He says that the servant had beaten a boy and he gives the name of the boy, his address, date of birth, the clothes he was wearing at the time, etc. This would furnish us with too many unnecessary details.

8. If we were to discuss all the finer touches this passage includes, we would be exceeding the limits of giving an example. Hence, we will only draw attention to a finer element unknown in ordinary speech. When a person is so keen to make a case, defending something or trying to persuade his audience, his speech is bound to reflect his emotions. We almost experience his feelings of pleasure when he succeeds and displeasure when he fails to achieve his purpose. If he is a keen believer in what he is preaching, he would take people's disinterest in what he says too much to heart. This is especially so with all prophets. Here, in the Qur'an, we do not fail to see something else: these are the words of a power that is too strong to be influenced by any such purpose.

There is an unmistakable dignity in stating clear arguments and giving precise descriptions. In arguing the case of the Qur'an, it simply describes it as *'the truth'*. The word is certainly full of meaning, but what human being is satisfied with using it in describing a fact which he wants people to believe in? Similarly, the passage records a most horrid crime perpetrated by the Jews when they considered the calf a deity to be worshipped. It then describes their hardened hearts as they refused to obey God's commandments, despite the clear proof that they had been shown. But when it describes these, it simply denounces the first as 'transgression', and the second as 'vile'. True, these terms adequately describe the offences when they are properly understood. But what human being would confine himself to such words when his status is held in question? What we find here is a dignified disputant that does not allow Himself to be drawn into a degrading argument. He is neither in need of gratitude nor affected by denial. These are the words of no human being.

Broadest Meaning, Minimum Wording

Chapter 9

> We have said that the Qur'an always invests the minimum possible wording to generate the broadest possible meaning. This is a common feature which is clearly noticeable throughout the Qur'an, in places which people describe as either calling for brevity or those that merit expansive elaboration. Hence, we describe the Qur'an as being concise throughout, because in both situations it does not add anything beyond what is absolutely necessary. Nor is it possible to express its meaning in either situation with a wording of shorter or equal length. Every single word it uses provides a key to a necessary and intrinsic meaning. Every letter fulfils a purpose.

We should discard altogether any talk about words being 'added unnecessarily' or particles being 'superfluous'. We should also discard any overuse of the word 'emphasis' which means that whenever a word is thought to be 'surplus', it is said to be 'added for emphasis.' Some people do that without thinking whether the place where it occurs requires or even permits emphasis. To give such a verdict on the Qur'an, describing it as using such 'surplus' words, is to betray ignorance of the fine and highly sensitive measures which constitute an essential element of the Qur'anic style.

When you have discarded all such claims, you should endeavour to fathom its literary merits in the light of what we have said earlier. If you do not readily understand the purpose of using a particular word or particle, do not jump to any conclusion like those who make claims of the type we

Broadest Meaning, Minimum Wording

have mentioned. You should say only what is wise and fair, such as: "God knows best the secrets of His own statements, and we only know what He has taught us." Do not be complacent and do not give up trying to discover its merits, saying that eminent literary figures have not been able to fathom it so nor can you. It is often the case that a person of lesser standing may be able to hit on something that has remained unnoticed by a more qualified specialist. The example of ᶜAbdullāh ibn ᶜUmar is well known. The Prophet once said to a group of his Companions who included such illustrious people as Abu Bakr and ᶜUmar: "There is a tree which does not discard its leaves. It is like a Muslim. Which tree is that?" They mentioned several types of tree, but none was the right answer. ᶜAbdullāh was the youngest among them and he felt it to be the date palm tree, but he kept quiet out of respect to his seniors. The Prophet then advised them: "It is the date palm tree."

It is, then, your duty to work hard and to pray to God to facilitate you with the acquisition of better knowledge. It may be that He will give you a breakthrough which will uncover what has remained unknown to others. It is He who *"brings the believers out of darkness into the light."* (2: 257.)

Let us take the example of the Qur'anic statement describing God Himself in these words: *"Naught is as His likeness."* (42: 11.) [This is the nearest and literal translation we can give to this sentence in order to capture its nuances. Most translators of the Qur'an render it as: "There is nothing like Him," but this is far from adequate.]

Most scholars agree that the particle 'as' is 'tautological' or 'redundant' here. Indeed many say that it is necessarily so. They feel that making it fully functional leads to a logical impossibility, as it would then negate comparison with God's likeness, not with God Himself. Thus, it would lead to admitting that there is, or there may be a 'peer' or an 'equal' to God. Logicians say that a negation affirms the opposite, while linguists say that negation may apply to what is qualified and what qualifies it as well. If you say, for example, 'ᶜAli has no son to help him', you may mean that he has no sons at all, or that he has a son but that son does not help him. Similarly, a statement like,

'Ḥasan is not a brother of ᶜAli', may mean either that Ḥasan has no brothers at all, or that he has a brother other than ᶜAli.

Some scholars say that 'as' may be considered as non-redundant if we say that it does not lead to such an impossibility in any linguistic sense. They say that negation of the likeness of a peer logically implies a negation of peers. They further say that if God has a peer, then that peer has, by necessity, an equal who is the true God Himself. Each one of any two peers is equal to his peer. Thus, the negation of an equal to a peer is impossible unless we negate parity in the first place. This is the intended meaning.

This interpretation, at best, provides a way out. It does nothing more than say that 'as' in the Qur'anic statement, *'Naught is as His likeness'*, causes no harm or confusion. It makes no attempt to show how it is useful and, indeed, necessary. When we consider this interpretation carefully we find that the meaning of the statement is the same whether it is used or not. Indeed, it only adds an element of pedantry and complication into the sentence. It is akin to someone who says: "This is the son of Mr X's maternal aunt's sister", instead of saying: "This is Mr X". In effect this interpretation makes 'as' redundant or superfluous, although it claims that it has an emphasising role. Indeed, there is no emphasis needed here. Besides, to emphasise a negation with a particle indicating likeness is essentially impossible.

Implicit Meanings in Abundance

If we reflect a little we find that this particle is highly significant, forming an essential part of the intended meaning. To omit it is to remove an aspect of the meaning which cannot be otherwise compensated for in the sentence. We will explain this in two ways, one more subtle than the other, hoping to bring out the meaning of this unusual statement in full relief.

The first, which is the easier to understand, is that if the Qur'anic verse were to simply say: "Nothing is like Him," then that would be a negation of

Broadest Meaning, Minimum Wording

an equal likeness, or a being who is exactly like Him. This is the meaning that comes to mind when we speak of likeness in general. If the statement was limited to this, then doubts might be raised that there could be a status which is not exactly the same as God's, but a degree below it. It may also be said that such a status belongs to angels and prophets, or to stars and natural forces, or to the *jinn*, idols and clergy. This would give such beings a similarity to God in His ability or knowledge, or a share in His creation or rule. But the use of 'as' in the sentence puts an end to all such doubts, as it removes the whole universe from any possibility of being like God, and of being similar to any shade of comparability with Him. It is as if the verse is saying: There is nothing which has any quality that brings it in any similarity with God, let alone it being similar to Him in reality. This is a case of highlighting what is inferior in order to stress what is superior. A similar case is the Divine order prohibiting the use of any words of offence when speaking to one's parents: "*Should one or both of them attain to old age in your care, never say 'Ugh' to them or chide them, but always speak gently and kindly to them.*" (17: 23.) This is an express order prohibiting the slightest offence, which means that a greater offence is even more strictly prohibited.

The second, which is more subtle, is that the immediate purpose of the verse, which is the negation of any comparability with God, is not all that the statement aims to convey. It would have been sufficient to state that negation by saying, 'Naught is like God,' or 'There is nothing like God'. But while the verse aims to emphasise this fact, it wants at the same time to draw our attentions to the logical argument that proves it.

If we wish to describe a certain person as having a good character and say, 'he is neither a liar nor miserly', we are simply making a statement without adding anything to prove it. But if we say, 'such a person is neither a liar nor miserly', we are not referring to a person similar to him and free of such unbecoming behaviour. Indeed, our statement in this case adds a universal proof of the absence of such qualities in his character. It denotes that a person with his fine qualities and benevolent character cannot be either a liar or a miserly. His good character will simply not admit such defects.

It is in the same way that the Qur'anic verse is phrased, so as to say that a being of such fine qualities as those of God can have none similar to him. Indeed, the universe cannot have two of His type. Hence, the statement employs two words, each denoting complete similarity, so as to use one of them as an essential part of the claim, while the other serves as an undeniable proof of the same claim. The negation of the similarity denoted by the particle, 'as', or '*ka*' in the Arabic text, signifies the complete uniqueness of God, while use of the word 'likeness', or '*mithl*' in Arabic, in reference to God Himself, alerts us to the indicated proof. This is, indeed, a special type of proof denoting the Oneness of the Creator in a way that no scholar of Divinity has, to our knowledge, ever approached. All the proofs they provide of God's Oneness seek to disprove the possibility of there being more than one deity by negating the practical results that form the outcome of such multiplicity. This is pointed out by the verse which says: "*Had there been in heaven or on earth any deities other than God, both [these realms] would surely have fallen into ruin.*" (21: 22.)

The argument here, which is the basis of all the points advanced by scholars of Divinity, is that a multiplicity of deities, each of whom having the qualities of the Divine Being, leads either to the non-existence of creatures, which means that they fall into ruin at the time of their existence, or leads to conflict between them that results in their falling into ruin after they are brought into existence. If we were to assume the presence of two gods and that both will for something to be created, they would not be able to do so because a single effect cannot be the result of two causes. To say that it is produced by the power of one of them while both have the same powers and forming the same will is to give one of them precedence over the other without any clear basis for it. On the other hand, if one of them wills to create something and the other wills to create its opposite, neither can be created because that would mean that two opposites exist concurrently at the same time and place. To allow one to be produced without the other is to demonstrate that one of them has precedence over the other. If one of these two gods wills to create some creatures different from those created by the

9. Broadest Meaning, Minimum Wording

other, then each deity will control his own sector of creation. This would mean the existence of two universes with a separate system for each. Inevitably, they will be in conflict until both are destroyed. All these possibilities are clearly disproved by the fact that the universe continues to exist following the same system. Every part of it functions harmoniously with the rest, like the organs of a single body function to serve the same purpose. This unity of operation is a proof of the Oneness of the Operator who orchestrates them all, [limitless is He in His glory].

All their arguments, then, are of the type pointed out by the verse quoted above, stating: *"Had there been in heaven or on earth any deities other than God, both [these realms] would surely have fallen into ruin."* The statement in *Surah* 42, *"Naught is as His likeness"*, looks at a meaning beyond this. It negates the very possibility of there being more than one God, regardless of any effects that such multiplicity produces. The verse is, thus, saying that the nature of Divinity is such that it differs from anything that accepts multiplicity or similarity with others. To admit such multiplicity or similarity is to make its perfection incomplete. But true Divinity presupposes absolute perfection negating the very concept of multiplicity or similarity.

The deeper you go in emphasising Divinity, the greater the superiority you imply, which means that the Divine Being is the origin of everything: *"It is He who is the Originator of the heavens and the earth."* (42: 11.) You also emphasise that He is in full control of everything: *"To Him belong the keys of the heavens and the earth."* (42: 12.) If you were to assume that these qualities apply to two beings, you contradict yourself most clearly. You simply make each one of the two beings superior and inferior, originator and originated, supreme and follower at the same time. Alternatively, you restrict their absolute perfection by making each one of them neither superior nor supreme in relation to the other. How, then, will either of them be God when *"to God belongs the essence of all that is most sublime in the heavens and the earth"*? (30: 27.)

We see now what a great contribution the particle 'as' adds to the meaning of the statement, *"Naught is as His likeness"*. It is useful to remember this example in order to appreciate the accuracy of the measure applied in the composition of the Qur'an.

A Difficult Approach Made Easy

But the secret of concise expression in the Qur'an is not limited to avoiding anything that is not essential to the meaning, or selecting the most expressive vocabulary which fits the purpose most clearly. The Qur'an employs an even harder and far more admirable method of keeping its wording to the absolute minimum.

At times we find the Qur'an, having omitted unnecessary additions and words that are not essential to the meaning, also leaves out some of the essential words without which the meaning is not normally properly conveyed. The deletion may affect many words and sentences that should either follow one another or come separately in the same passage. It then invests the vocabulary that remains in conveying the whole meaning clearly, accurately and in fine style. In fact, it appears that the wording makes such a full expression of the meaning that we may think that the wording is more than adequate for the meaning intended.

If you look for the secret in all this, you will find that it places the meaning of the deleted words and sentences in a word here and a particle there. It then fashions its style with dexterity so as to make the outcome most fitting for the purpose. Furthermore, it brings out its finer elements in sharp relief so as to make the style most coherent and expressive. It breathes life into it making it smooth, easy, bright and enlightening. As we read, we do not feel what deletions and omissions have taken place, nor do we appreciate how the meaning is adequately and fully expressed unless we examine it very carefully.

9. Broadest Meaning, Minimum Wording

There is no doubt that the Arabs used to resort to some omission in their speech, considering it to be a literary virtue, provided that there was sufficient indication pointing to what was deleted, even though it may have been essential to the sentence. When an Arab is asked, 'Where is your brother?' he may say, 'at home'. And if he is asked, 'Who is at home', he would say, 'My brother'. If he were to answer either question by saying, 'My brother is at home', his answer would be felt to be unnecessarily verbose. In this aspect, like in all aspects of literary expression, the Qur'an attains a height too sublime for human talent, unattainable even in our wildest dreams.

Let us take this example: "*If God were to hasten for human beings the ill in the same manner as they would hasten the good, their end would indeed come forthwith! But We leave those who do not believe that they are destined to meet Us in their overweening arrogance, blindly stumbling to and fro.*" (10: 11.) [This rendering leaves out all that translators of the Qur'an add in parentheses to capture the meaning.]

This verse speaks of those who reject the concept of resurrection and whom the Prophet informed of his message telling them that he was a warner to them against an impending and painful suffering. They ridiculed him and said: "*God, if this is indeed the truth from You, then rain down upon us stones from the skies, or inflict [some other] grievous suffering on us.*" (8: 32.) God, however, has not done what they suggested, but instead has delayed their punishment to the time He has appointed. They felt secure in the life of peace they were enjoying and forgot that time brings all sorts of misfortune. They overlooked the fact that God may inflict His punishment on them at any time. Essentially, this led them to hasten such evil, just like people are eager to receive what is of benefit to them immediately. They started to say: When will it be? What stops it from coming if it is true?

The Qur'an wants to reply to this by saying that if it was God's law to respond to people when they hasten what is evil in the same way as He responds to them when they hasten good, He would have hastened it to them. But it is His unchangeable law that He gives respite to the transgressors and defers reckoning their actions, good or bad, to the time He has appointed. The law will operate in the case of those people so as to give them respite until their appointed time. This is the nature of the reply as it may be expressed in human language. Now let us look at what happens to it when it is stated in the Qur'an.

1. Taken in its ordinary form, the argument has three elements: two serve as introductory and the third as a conclusion. The Qur'an states the first and the third, while the second is left out. Thus, it is only implied.

2. The first introduction in its idle state has four ingredients: God's hastening good and evil, and people's request for both to be hastened. But in the verse we see only one hastening from God and one demand for haste from people.

3. The apparent contrast is in the similarity of one type of haste and another, or one type of request for haste and another. The verse is phrased rather strangely so as to draw the similarity between one element from the first set [i.e. haste] and an element from the second set [i.e. hastening request].

But after all this deletion and modification do we find the text to be incomplete or twisted or not readily understood? Or do we find the whole import of the verse to be clear to all and sundry, like a full moon on a clear night? It is useful to dig into the secrets of fine style and ask how the meaning is so clear despite all this economy of expression?

In comment on all three points outlined above we say firstly that the verse has only deleted the implied introductory element after it has raised two banners on its two sides to indicate its presence and transmit it to us clearly. To its right, it has placed the negative conditional, 'if God were...' at the beginning of the first introduction. This implies that God does not hasten such matters. To its left, it has placed the Arabic particle, '*fa*', which is rendered in the translation as 'but'. This implies a detail indicating a normal state of affairs. The meaning implied here is that 'it is His practice that He leaves

Broadest Meaning, Minimum Wording

people to carry on with what they choose for themselves. Hence, He leaves the people to whom the verse refers until their appointed time arrives.'

But the Arabic particle, *fa*, on its own does not specifically denote what is intended, because it is frequently used as a conjunction. Thus, a reader may read it as though it serves as a conjunction here before he realises that it is not so. To avoid this, the Qur'an does not rely on this particle alone, but adds two supporting forces in the form of changing tense from past to present, and changing the referent from the third person to the first. This causes a verbal break between it and the preceding sentence. This break echoes a similar break in meaning, inviting a complete pause before it. This ensures that no confusion or ambiguity is felt by the reader or the listener. Moreover, this change of tense and person alerts the listener and makes the warning much more effective, coming as it does from God, the Almighty Himself.

As for the second point we note that when the omission applied to two of the four ingredients, it is made to apply to both aspects, taking out one ingredient from each and leaving the other. The parallel in this process indicates the presence of what has been deleted.

The third point identifies a fine aspect of the meaning indicating the reason for giving respite and why God does not hasten punishment. The verse portrays this hastening as though the person requesting it is so keen to have what he requests to be hastened because it will satisfy a burning desire, particularly if he is seeking what is certain to benefit him. Thus, the verse implies that if God were to hasten what they are demanding, He would be in the same position as those precipitating matters, as He would be provoked into it. Far be it from God to be so.

Yet there are more artistic touches in the text of the verse. One of these is that usually the particular conditional conjunction used here is peculiar to Arabic and should normally be followed by a verb in the past tense. But the purpose here is not to negate a past occurrence. It is to explain that what the unbelievers hasten is contrary to the laws of nature God has set in operation in human life. Such laws are valid for all time, without change. To put this meaning in normal style, longer language would have been needed, such as: 'Had it been the normal law God has set for human life that He should hasten, etc.'. But all this is summed up in one word through the use of the present tense, which implies repetition and continuity. The conditional conjunction is used to indicate that what follows it refers to a past event. Thus, the time of the occurrence and its continuous nature are gently pushed to the fore.

The second touch is seen in the phraseology of the conditional sentence. Normally, the second part of a conditional should tie up with its first part. This would have meant that the sentence should be phrased like this: "If God were to hasten for human beings the ill... He would have hastened it, etc.". But this is discarded in preference for something far more telling and effective. The verse explains that had God wanted to hasten an evil outcome to people, He would have hastened for that particular community a special type of hard suffering which would make their end occur forthwith.

Yet we see another touch in the way the verse is ended. The logical conclusion of the verse should probably have been something like, 'But We leave them', or 'But We leave these people'. The verse, however, runs as follows: *"If God were to hasten for human beings the ill in the same manner as they would hasten the good, their end would indeed come forthwith! But We leave those who do not believe that they are destined to meet Us in their overweening arrogance, blindly stumbling to and fro."* In this way, it accomplishes an important dual purpose. First, it makes it clear that their hastening of evil is due to the fact that they do not believe in resurrection. It also shows that granting respite is the general rule which applies to them and others like them.

The verse has other touches, but we will leave these for now. We only say that we may find one type of these dextrous manipulations in the style of any literary figure, but what human being displays in his or her style all these aspects, or a similar set in a passage of the same length, or even in one twice as long?

Broadest Meaning, Minimum Wording

Let us take another example tackling the same thought: "*Say: Have you ever considered if His punishment were to befall you by night or by day? What could there be in such prospect that people lost in sin should wish to hasten? Is it, then, that you will believe in it [only] after it has come to pass? Is it now [you believe in it], after having called for its speedy advent?*" (11: 50-51.)

If we were to paraphrase these two verses, we may say that what God is saying goes as follows: "Tell me what will your situation be, should God's punishment befall you all of a sudden, at night or during the day. What will you do then? You have one of two choices: either you persist with what you are doing now, continuing to deny God's message and hasten the result that may take place, or you accept the faith. Which of these would you choose? Will you still ask for the punishment to be hastened then as you hasten it now? Certainly not, because you are sinners, and a sinner will never look forward to the punishment that is bound to overwhelm him once it is decided. Besides, what type of punishment are you trying to speed up? You should know that it differs in type and severity. Or is it that you deny it today, then when it comes about in due course you will believe in it? Let me tell you that such a belief will not be of any benefit to you, since you have delayed and procrastinated so long that the time for it has gone. You will be reproached and told: is it now that you want to believe while you were always denying that punishment and challenging us to hasten it."

This is the meaning conveyed in these two verses. We only need to look at them carefully to see how many sentences have been left as implied at the beginning, middle and end. But for everything that is deleted, the verses include a clue to point to it or a mark showing it. In the first verse, we have two interrogative sentences indicating that a comprehensive question is made up of the two, asking: What will you do, and which course will you follow? The interrogative about the type of punishment being hastened indicates an earlier and preliminary question about the very idea of hastening it. The reference to those '*lost in sin*' implies that it is impossible for what this part of the verse refers to, i.e. the hastening of punishment, to take place, because they will be its recipients. There are many other words or phrases deleted from the text, but clearly understood. This could only happen in the Qur'an with its unique style. Indeed, no one has ever attempted to combine such brevity of style and word economy with such clarity of meaning without soon finding himself in deep water, unable to proceed after the first hurdle. Indeed, to achieve such an aim requires far more effort than anyone could put in. This should tell us much about the real challenge of the Qur'an.

Chapter 10

The Unity of Each *Surah*

We have highlighted the richness of meaning in the Qur'anic style, despite its unparalleled word economy. But we have to add to that another aspect which gives its wealth of meaning its best adornment, bringing out its beauty in full splendour. This aspect is the perfect coherence of all its constituent elements and the firm bonding of all its parts which make of it a single unit that cannot be split up.

We all know that when a single subject is treated in poor style, its unity of meaning is loosened. Thus, it becomes disjointed and lacking in coherence, just like an image reflected in a mirror becomes broken when the mirror has an uneven surface. After all, words form a mirror reflecting the meaning they convey. Hence, bringing out the natural unity of meaning requires proper literary and artistic coherence. This is achieved through matching the elements used in literary expression so that they can be consolidated into a complete whole.

This is by no means easy, as may be imagined by those who are unaware of what literary refinement means. In fact, it is a hard task requiring skill and dexterity, as well as a fine sense that enables a writer to determine the best position for each part: which should be a main theme and which is to be treated as complementary; which should be placed at the beginning, which forms the conclusion and which occupies the centre position. The writer is also required to choose the best methods to put these parts together, and when to use gradual progression, straight conjunction, or other methods of

10 The Unity of Each *Surah*

joining. But all this comes after the parts themselves have been carefully selected, making sure that each one of them is closely related to the overall meaning and free of alien or unnecessary aspects. He should also make sure that both ends and the middle of each part are of equal relevance to the overall purpose of the writer's piece of work, and that the theme being treated is equally relevant to all these parts. It is a case similar to a circle where every point is of equal distance from the centre.

All this applies to a single theme with a natural link between all its constituent parts. How is it, then, when the discussion tackles several themes that vary in essence and substance and have naturally unrelated parts? How much skill and talent, or indeed what magical touches, are required to bring about a measure of coherence between their diverse natures and separate courses, so that when they are brought together in discussion they do not appear to be like an assortment that puts together a pen, a pair of shoes, a saw and a bucket of water? What sort of talent will bring them together in one line of discussion, enabling their smaller details to unite in an all-embracing and closely-knit whole?

The difficulty of this goal has practically placed it beyond the reach of the best literary talents. Great literary figures may attain different degrees of excellence when they take up one issue at a time. But when they seek to tackle different themes in the same piece of work, they fall into error and betray inadequacy. When poets attempt different themes in the same poem, they often treat these separately or at random. It is rarely the case that they manage to achieve an easy, flowing switch from one theme to another, such as moving from love poetry to praise, both of which were standard themes of Arabic poetry. They often use tools designed to alert the listener to the change of theme, or they talk in the first person. Hence, we often encounter alerting words, such as, 'however, moreover, besides, but, etc.' or phrases like, 'be that as it may…; having said that…; let us now discuss…; we now move to…, etc.'.

This is the case when different themes are tackled in the same discourse on the same occasion. What sort of treatment would we have, should they be treated on different occasions, separated by lengthy time intervals? It is only to be expected that the links would be very difficult to put in place and the gaps all the more apparent.

If we admire the literary excellence of the Qur'an in a short passage, with a single theme that is naturally coherent, let us now consider the Qur'anic style over a whole surah, which includes different topics and themes, with different passages being revealed on different occasions and in varying circumstances. Here, we will find the consistency of style and the unity of subject matter at their most wonderful.

The importance the Qur'anic style attaches to brevity and concise expression, always avoiding lengthy discourse, as far as that is feasible while maintaining a superbly fine style, has made it the most innovative discourse we will ever come across. By innovative we mean that it employs a wide variety of styles and moves from one to the other at a speed unrivalled by any other discourse. Thus, it employs description, narration, legislative text, argument and many other forms. Indeed, it goes further than that so as to use the same style in a variety of ways, making it a group of styles.

What is even more remarkable is that despite being the most varied discourse in its themes and subjects, the Qur'an is also most innovative in style when discussing a single subject. It neither retains the same mode for long, nor does it continue to address the same theme for any unnecessary length. Indeed, as it changes themes within the same surah, it employs different modes, such as implicit or explicit statements, narrative, nominal or verbal sentences, past, present or future tenses, first, second or third person, etc. The speed of switch from one mode to the other is such that it is totally unknown in any other style. Such rapid and frequent switching normally leads to confusion or error both in treating a subject and in moving from one subject to the other. But at no time do we ever detect such confusion or error in the Qur'an. Indeed, it maintains a superb standard of powerful,

The Unity of Each *Surah*

flawless style throughout, utilising all these modes in painting a magnificent scene in which nothing is felt to be out of place. What person, having a good command of Arabic, makes a thorough study of the Qur'anic style without finding in its construction an aspect of the Qur'anic challenge?

Some newcomers to the study of the beauty of the Qur'anic style and its powerful construction may wonder about the psychological ease experienced by both the reciter of the Qur'an and its listener. It gives them both new freshness and renewed interest at every stage, so as never to be bored no matter how long they continue with their reading or listening. This peculiar phenomenon has different sources in the Qur'an. We referred to some of these when we discussed the unique sound characteristics of the Qur'an in Chapter VIII. But this psychological ease has an even deeper and more profound source, which is best appreciated by one who has studied fine speech thoroughly, distinguishing the finer qualities of literary works and how resourceful authors make use of their talents to produce their fine pieces. As such a person compares their styles with the Qur'an, he realises that even the finest of talented poets and writers remain at the lowest step of a long ladder while the Qur'an attains the zenith. Indeed, when the Qur'an moves from one stage to another, it gives in the new stage several new aspects of the theme it discusses and the style it employs. With such a continuous process of renewal, how can any reader or listener be bored?

We can always try for ourselves, when we stand for a long while contemplating the same beautiful scene: does that give us the same sensation and admiration as a series of beautiful scenes, portraying different aspects of fine arrangement and splendid scenery? Certainly not! The same applies to the Qur'anic style, which is so varied and continuously changing.

It is well known that, for the most part, the process of revelation of the Qur'an is not one that brings different themes all at the same time. On the contrary, these themes were revealed individually, on numerous occasions, as required by events and needs. These differences of time and occasion would have, by necessity, meant that the themes discussed should have resulted in a sort of separate and independent treatment on each occasion, leaving no room for linkages and cohesion.

These two reasons, the rapid and continuous change of style and mode of expression on the one hand and the tackling of different themes on separate occasions on the other, should have worked together in creating inconsistency and disjointedness when the separate revelations were joined together in the same surah.

Take, if you will, the text of a number of statements by the Prophet, or by any person of great literary talent, tackling different themes and which are known to have been made on different occasions. Then try to read them together, one after the other, in the same way as you read a single speech, without adding or omitting anything of them. We do not need too long to realise that neither their meanings nor their texts would be consistent with one another. On the contrary, they would clearly betray a degree of discrepancy and patching up that is hardly ever noticed in a single speech, of similar or greater length.

Final Arrangement Made Far in Advance

Another reason which should have made a surah appear particularly disjointed is the way in which the Qur'an joins different parts together in order to establish the unity of each surah. This provides a third most remarkable aspect that puts the Qur'an in a class apart from all human styles, old and new.

What does a person do when he wants to make a product in which he needs to use several parts and components? The first thing is to review the parts and components at his disposal, making sure how they fit together, before making a plan that determines the place of every one of them. Making a plan cannot precede the finding out of the material at one's disposal; in the same way that a picture cannot be taken of what is unseen. To reverse these

10 The Unity of Each *Surah*

two steps is to force the human mind along an unfamiliar, very slippery way, without providing any sort of guidance. Have you ever seen anyone following such an unnatural route and managing to achieve his objective without difficulty?

Would any rational human being determine the exact position of every part of what he wants to produce before making sure what parts he has at his disposal and the exact measurements and qualities of each part? Should he start with such determination, would his initial decision be his final one, subject to no change or review? If he insists on following such a method, will he manage to achieve the sort of perfection a master craftsman aspires to achieve? No intelligent person would ever do that. If he does it in respect of certain stages of his work, relying on his intuition, his plan remains provisional. He will be ready to change it the moment he realises that a change is necessary or desirable. He will then go back to modify his first plan marginally here, substantially there, shifting an important component from one stage to another, or using it as a separate stage altogether. He will continue to review his material and modify his overall plan time and again until he comes up with a final version that uses each part in its most suitable place. Any arrangement that uses the parts before making sure of the available material will be arbitrary, giving only an incomplete picture. The same applies to any structure that is not worked out on the basis of complete and detailed knowledge of its parts. It will remain flimsy, liable to collapse at any time.

In fact when a human being begins to put together the components of any matter, he has to follow the natural way that determines the direction of anyone who has a definite objective in mind, whether physical or logical. If he needs to cover a number of steps, or climb upstairs, he simply cannot take a later step before he completes the preceding one, in the same way as he cannot climb a higher flight of stairs before a lower one. All this is determined by nature and applies to all our material and intellectual products. The rules apply in the same way to a builder, tailor, writer and poet.

Consider, if you will, this example. Suppose a man arrives in a vast plain where there is neither a building of any sort nor any building materials. Suddenly he feels an earthquake or a storm, and sees the top of a nearby mountain opening up and casting off some rocks and stones. After a short or long interval a similar event takes place, giving him a reasonable amount of iron, or silver or gold fragments. Do you think that any rational human being in this position would immediately resolve to build a whole town, using the material he has and that which he expects as a result of similar quakes and storms? Would he immediately begin to put his plan into effect and start the building process? How can he be certain that the phenomena that gave him the initial material will happen again? If it does, how often? What sort of material would it give him every time, and in what quantities? How many buildings will it be possible for him to build, and in what system? How spacious will each building be? How many floors will it have? In what finish and decoration will it be? How much land is available to him for building?

In such total uncertainty, no rational human being would plan to build a small hut, let alone a large town. He would certainly not start to build as soon as he received his first few rocks.

Let us now imagine that a person will nevertheless undertake such an adventure, and that fate gives him what he needs of building materials to complete the project he has devised. Would he undertake another adventure, following an unnatural method of building, vowing to place each brick or stone he receives in its ultimate place, wherever that might happen to be, the moment he gets hold of it? Would he do that when he knows for certain that the bricks he receives come in various forms, sizes and strengths; some are light while others are heavy; and arrive in no definite order. He may have the material to be used in the terrace or the balcony before he receives the posts and beams that support the basic structure. He may have, at the same time, several incomplete parts to be used wide apart. Should he try to place each small part in its ultimate place the moment he gets it, that would inevitably give him scattered, incomplete and unrelated parts, with varying distances

10 The Unity of Each Surah

in between. He would have to bring some bits together while others be kept separate. He may even try to build the loft of one building before he lays its foundation, or start with the ceiling without first raising its support.

How can any human being embark on such an adventure and carry on with it to its completion without going back at any moment to amend his plan or move any part from its original position to a new, seemingly better one, or to give any part more support or new decoration? How is it possible that the moment he lays the last brick or strikes the last nail, we see a complete town, perfectly planned, with every palace, home, room, or brick right in its most suitable position, adding to the beauty of the whole construction. Should any part or substance be moved from its place, a defect will be noticeable. Does that not constitute a huge challenge to the whole human race?

Planning the Whole Prior to Receiving the Parts

Yet this has actually happened in the matter we are considering. The man in our example is the Prophet (peace be upon him), who was never taught how to read and write. The great city which he began to build ever since its first bricks were given to him is this perfect book, the Qur'an. Ever since he received its early verses, he started to arrange its parts, confident that it would undoubtedly produce a complete and perfect whole. The palaces, rooms and bricks in our example are the surahs, passages and verses of the Qur'an.

The unexpected events that brought the man in our example the rocks and metals that went into the building of palaces and villas are the world events, social developments and religious and worldly problems that faced people time after time in their private or public affairs. A believer would ask about these to learn what he should know. A non-believer would use them to argue and dispute. In all these events Qur'anic revelations were given, a passage at a time, treating meanings that differed widely as would suit each case or occasion, in different lengths, and with varying tones ranging from the very lenient to the stiff and very hard. From these widely different passages, the sets known as surahs were formed, not on the basis of compatibility in each set, but allowing any number of passages, addressing any questions to join any set.

The totally unusual method followed in raising those buildings of the city in our example, haphazardly using their constituent parts, which is the third factor that makes the task impossible rather than hard, is also seen clearly in the Qur'an. The man who received its revelations did not wait until all its passages had been given to him. Indeed, he did not wait for a single surah to be completed before deciding on its arrangement. Whenever he received a passage or a single verse, he ordered that it should be placed in its particular slot in a well-defined position in its surah.

We should emphasise here that the revelation of verses and passages did not follow the order in which they occur in the Qur'an. Many a surah was revealed, in whole or in parts, interspersed with the revelation of other passages in different surahs. Many a verse is placed towards the end of a surah despite its being revealed much earlier than the parts preceding it, and vice versa. Indeed, the revelation and arrangement of Qur'anic verses and passages were two separate matters following two different routes which hardly ever met. This gives us a profoundly edifying aspect of the arrangement of this unique book.

If we look at each passage at the time of its revelation, and study the different aspects associated with its revelation: its timing, the events leading to it and the needs it satisfies, we are certain to conclude that each was topical at its particular time of revelation. Each one addressed a matter that happened to exist at a particular time. Prior to the event concerned, there was no indication suggesting that it was forthcoming. Hence, each passage is a complete whole that does not follow a pattern which puts it with other passages in a particular mould.

10 The Unity of Each *Surah*

Let us at the same time consider how each passage is placed at the very moment of its revelation within a particular framework which either has been set in advance, or will be set at a later stage, and given a definite slot that occurs early or late within that framework. At the time of its revelation, a passage is ordered to be placed, say, at the end of a particular surah, while another passage, revealed after a short or long while, is placed in the same surah, after a given number of its verses. One passage may be ordered to be placed at the outset of a surah of which no part has yet been revealed, while a subsequent passage is placed within a surah the rest of which has long since been revealed.

When we consider such detailed instructions on the arrangement of passages and surahs we are bound to conclude that there is a complete and detailed plan assigning the position of each passage before they are all revealed. Indeed the arrangement is made before the reasons leading to the revelation of any passage occur, and even before the start of the preliminary causes of such events. Nevertheless, this whole, meticulously detailed plan of distribution and arrangement was made with full resolve and determination. Not a single verse or passage placed in a particular surah was later moved to a different one. Nor was a verse placed at the beginning or the end of a surah ever re-assigned a different position in that same surah at a later stage.

Such are the plain facts about the arrangement of the Qur'an as it was revealed in separate verses, passages and surahs over a period of 23 years. What does this tell us about its source?

An Arrangement Pointing Out the Author

When we consider carefully the timing of the revelation of the Qur'anic passages and surahs and their arrangement, we are profoundly astonished. We almost belie what we see and hear. We then begin to ask ourselves for an explanation of this highly improbable phenomenon: is it not true that this new passage of revelation has just been heard as new, addressing a particular event which is its only concern? Yet it sounds as though it is neither new nor separate from the rest. It seems as if it has been, along with the rest of the Qur'an, perfectly impressed on this man's mind long before he has recited it to us. It has been fully engraved on his heart before its composition in the words he recites. How else can it unite so perfectly and harmoniously parts and pieces that do not naturally come together?

Why has the person receiving these passages not left them separate as they were initially revealed? And when he decided to group them together, why has he not made of them a single set? Or put them in equal or similar sets? What basis has he followed in their collation, distribution and arrangement in the present fashion, before they were complete in full or in part? Can all this be by mere coincidence? Certainly not; for each situation is clearly intended as it is. The deliberate intention is also clear that every group of passages or verses should be joined together in a separate unit of a particular length and arrangement. Or is it possible that all these arrangements, intended as they may be, do not follow a pre-determined order, but have come about as a result of an experiment that follows a spontaneous thought? That could not be the case. When each part was put in its position, the one who placed them never had a new thought or introduced any modification or re-arrangement. How then could he have determined his plan? And how could he have made his intention so clear in advance?

That is the line of questioning that we may ask ourselves. When we listen attentively to the logical answer, it will have to run in the following fashion: A person who dares to make such a detailed and perfectly planned design must be either a deeply ignorant one or one who has perfect and absolute knowledge that transcends human logic. There can be no other alternative. If he is one who has completed its perfect system of composition and arrangement before he has had complete and confirmed knowledge of the reasons behind the composition of each passage, its purpose, objectives and what it entails, then he merely resorts to guesswork and random preference. Such a person is a shameless impudent who dares to claim for himself what

10 The Unity of Each *Surah*

he does not have. His vain boasting will soon prove to be otiose. You only need to leave him alone for a while and the fallacy of his position will be made clearly apparent. It is not possible that ignorance should give birth to a solid system that lasts and flourishes.

If, on the other hand, this person has made his design on the basis of infallible knowledge, placing every verse and every passage in its perfectly designed position, then the system he comes up with must be unquestionably perfect and splendidly beautiful. But then the designer cannot be that human being, unless it has been imparted to him by a source well beyond his highest horizon. How is it possible for a human being, subject as he is to the effect of time, to be in control of the nature of time? When a human being is completely ignorant of the causes and preliminaries of his action, can he be well aware of the details of its results and consequences? Can he be completely unaware, yet perfectly aware, of the one and same thing? Is it possible that he should be subject to, and in control of, the same thing, at the same time?

Has anyone ever seen or heard that a poet or a man of letters was able at the start of his literary career to collect all that he would ever say or write of poetry or prose on all future occasions right to the point of his death. He would then devise a plan for his future edition of his complete works which does not merely predict their themes and chapters, but perfectly estimates the number of poems and articles that each theme and chapter will include and defines for each future poem and article its exact position in the ultimate edition. Then when in his future life the time arrives for any such work to be produced, he would put it in its pre-defined position without question. What is more is that his plan would score an unqualified success, showing the wisdom of his planning and fulfilling his dreams. His system will appear to all and sundry to be perfect, putting all his future works in their respective pre-arranged positions, changing nothing and modifying nothing.

If such a hypothesis can ever be true of anyone, it will be true of the Prophet who delivered the Qur'an. But man remains what he is. A human being who is totally unaware of future events in his life that will prompt him to express his thoughts in prose or poetry is less likely to be aware of the actual text of what he will say, and further unlikely to know the merit of each text. Indeed, when a person feels the urge to compose something, he will choose one of two options. The first is to leave his thought as he has expressed it. He does the same with what he writes or says on subsequent occasions. When he has composed enough material, he goes back to what he has written, putting like with like, separating what needs to be put apart, classifying and arranging his work in a suitable and coherent order. The second option is to gather these texts according to their chronological order.

There is a third option, which is to leave them in groups. He will then work on each group separately, putting its parts together in a rigid and haphazard way, not allowing any piece to be shifted from its original place. He will still hope that in this way, he will come up with a well ordered and classified work, perfectly arranged into parts and chapters. What is more is that his work will show an unusual degree of coherence that puts every sentence, word and particle in its right place. Such an option will only produce the opposite of what one desires.

Perfect Unity of Whole and Part

We have seen how human beings work when they try to produce a coherent whole out of separate parts, whether this be a literary piece or something different. This is totally different from the unity that is produced when parts of Qur'anic revelations are joined together to form a single whole. Indeed, the Qur'anic order should have reflected absolutely no unity or coherence because of three different factors that should have made it totally disjointed. These are: divergent elements of the meaning, times of revelation separated by long or short periods, and widely different situations to be addressed on each occasion.

10 The Unity of Each *Surah*

Let us now consider whether these factors and their combined effect have diminished in any way the coherent order of any surah that has been composed in such a manner. The Arabs who were challenged to produce a single surah like the Qur'an would have jumped at the opportunity to detract from the Qur'an, had they found any flaw in the composition of a single surah. They would have needed no temptation to have a go at it. Literary critics of the highest calibre in successive generations have been citing examples from the Qur'an to illustrate perfect harmony of composition when it addresses different meanings or changes styles and modes of expression.

We for our part should study carefully the construction of the Qur'an and how its arrangement has been made so as to produce such a perfect structure to merit God's description of it: "*A discourse in the Arabic tongue, free of all deviousness.*" (39: 28.) Take any one of the many surahs of the Qur'an that tackle more than one purpose. Indeed, these are the majority. Now review it very carefully, stage by stage, and then contemplate it again, and yet again: how it begins, and how it ends. How it reflects the contrast and balance between its constituent parts. How it relates its main themes to each other. And how its premises lead to its conclusions, and the early parts lead to those that follow.

I maintain that no one will ever find in the line of the meanings it portrays or in the construction of its verses and sentences anything to indicate whether it was revealed all on the same occasion or on several occasions. You will imagine that each one of the seven longest *surahs* was revealed in total on one occasion, but then you will have to acknowledge the fact that all or most of them were revealed one passage at a time. In fact, this applies to all *surahs*, long and short as they may be, which have been revealed in parts. In fact, very short surahs, like surahs 93, 96 and 107 were each revealed in two parts, on two different occasions. Of the longest seven surahs, perhaps Surah 6 was revealed on one occasion, as scholars suggest. But then the method of moving from one meaning to another in Surah 6 and the surahs revealed on several occasions is the same.

It may be said that although a surah might have been put together after its parts were revealed separately, these parts were in one whole unit prior to their separate revelation. This would be the same as, say, a historic building which needs to be moved as it is from one place to another. Its detailed dimensions are measured and its every stone or brick is given a number before it is dismantled. In this way, every little part is assigned its exact position. When it is reconstructed, it regains its exact shape and acquires an even more solid foundation.

When we read a long surah that was revealed in a number of passages over a long period of time, an ignorant person may think that it is no more than an assortment of laboured meanings and a random collection of syntactic structures. But when you examine it very carefully you will find it to be a solid structure bringing together the main purposes in an elaborate system which lays down every aspect, giving it its sections and branches which are then further divided into long or short subdivisions. When you move from one part of the surah to another, you feel as if you are looking at the rooms and halls of one building that has been designed by a single architect who gave it his whole attention until the building was completed. You will not feel any mismatch in the allocation of space or the distribution of amenities. Nor will you sense any split as you move from one passage to another. Indeed, the reverse is true. You will feel perfect unity between the different types and consummate harmony between the constituent parts of each type. What is more is that all this has been achieved without recourse to anything apart from the intended purposes themselves. What helps to bring it about are the ease of introduction and the fine treatment at the beginning, middle and completion of every purpose. Thus, you see a direct link between separate parts and perfect harmony between distinct identities.

But then we do not give a proper description of the unity of the Qur'anic surahs when we compare them to a single building with rooms and halls conforming to the same design. This is an inadequate description. The parts and passages of each surah are welded together and brought into perfect

The Unity of Each *Surah*

harmony in the same way as the organs of the human body. Between each two passages there is an inherent link uniting them together, in the same way as two bones meet at a joint with a mass of connective tissues and ligaments completing the linkage, then the two organs supported by the two bones are linked by arteries and nerves. Beyond that, the whole surah moves in the same direction to fulfil a particular purpose, just like we see the human body having a single stature, while all its organs perform different biological functions that help to complete a single purpose.

Remember that the parts and elements that ensure the unity of each surah were related to events that had not all taken place at the time of the revelation of that surah in the Qur'an, nor were they expected to happen at the outset of its revelation. Moreover, the perfection of that unity required that all these events and causes must, by necessity, take place at their appointed and allocated time so that the Qur'an might have the opportunity to address them. The question that must be asked here is: what dictated the course of events so as to make it serve the purpose of these passages and to ensure that every single event should take place at the time of the revelation of the Qur'an? Should a single event have failed to materialise at the time, the whole system giving the Qur'an its unity and harmony would have been disrupted. This would have given us at least one surah without a proper opening or conclusion, or with a split in the middle.

The fact that cosmic events have been made to serve the structure of these literary passages and ensure their perfect unity provides clear evidence that both the literary speech and the actual event have come from the same source. Indeed, the One whose knowledge has given these words is the One whose will has produced those events and creatures. They are all from God, whose will is always done and whose verdict is final. All glory belongs to Him.

The Details and the Whole in the Qur'anic Picture

Let us now suppose that the man who has given us the Qur'an could have been able to predict with perfect accuracy all future events, important and trivial, that would take place through the remainder of his own life. Let us further imagine that he was also able to determine what teachings of the Qur'an would be needed to address these future events. The question to be asked here is: how could he have known the literary design that these teachings would take? How could he have predicted which teachings would go with which parts and passages, so as to be ready to receive each part as it is revealed and give it its appropriate and firm link that fits it most perfectly in its pre-assigned slot? How come that when each passage was revealed it found itself in its most suitable position, perfectly comfortable with its adjoining parts. The space assigned to it is neither too narrow to give a laboured impression, nor too loose to weaken its links with the rest. It fits in like the final piece in a jigsaw puzzle. There was never a need to make even the slightest change, or rearrangement, or to delete or add even a particle in the preceding passage to allow the new one to slot in.

Indeed, how could that man have known each part and to what unit or group it belonged? How could he have known at what position in that unit it would be placed, well before he became aware of the other parts of the unit? How is it that when the separate parts given at random are all set in their respective positions, assigned to them in advance, the curtain is raised and we see every surah like a beauty queen, perfectly moulded, tastefully adorned?

What elaborate design, what perfect forethought, and what faultless knowledge that never forgets, hesitates or errs, has prepared for such a broad assortment of material its perfect design, and directed each piece of it to its assigned slot? How come that when each has taken its place according to the advance design, the result is a necklace in which each gemstone is perfectly placed so as to add to the superb beauty of the necklace while losing nothing of its own attraction.

10. The Unity of Each *Surah*

We all know that human knowledge always looks at what it has completed and says: 'If I were to begin anew, I would have changed this plan for that, or started with this idea instead of that'. Such knowledge simply cannot produce a perfect design in advance of the events to which it applies. This, in itself, is an irrefutable proof that the Qur'an is made by no human being. Its author is the One whose knowledge is perfect, absolute and independent of time. *"Had [the Qur'an] issued from any but God, they would surely have found in it many an inner contradiction."* (4: 82.)

We need now to provide a proof of what we have stated, and give an example of the unity of each surah, despite all factors that should have militated against such unity. We will show how a single surah revealed in parts over a long period of time becomes like a chain of ideas with one ring leading to the next in an easily flowing system in which words, sentences and verses are inseparably welded. The best example to give is the longest surah in the Qur'an, with the broadest variety of meaning and purpose, expressed in the largest number of passages and revealed over the longest period of time. This is the second surah of the Qur'an, comprising 286 verses, constituting, according to the occasions of its revelation, more than 80 passages, revealed over a period of nine years. It mentions the change of the direction we face in Prayer, i.e the *qiblah*, and the order to fast in the month of Ramadhan, and comments on the first military clash in the history of Islam. All these were revealed early in the second year after the Prophet's settlement in Madinah. It also contains the last verse ever to be revealed of the Qur'an: *"Fear the day when you shall all return to God, when every soul shall be repaid in full for what it has earned, and none shall be wronged."* (2: 281.)

It is not our purpose here to point out the verbal and mental linkages that join the parts of this surah. That is a detailed study, better suited for a full commentary on the Qur'an. Yet it is possible to outline in a single part of the *surah* links and bonds stretched out in all directions, related to close and distant parts and forming a network of connective threads that leave us wondering which to follow first, and which is meant to provide the first bond.

What we propose to do instead is to look at the whole surah in a systematic way tracing how it proceeds from start to finish and highlighting the unity of its overall semantic structure. This will show us how every ring is tied in its right position in that long chain. However, before we embark on our plan we should say that such a study as we will be undertaking should be the first step in a careful review of the Qur'anic structure and arrangement. A detailed study of the links found at the beginning and within verses and passages should only be undertaken after one has looked at the whole surah, determined its parts and identified its purposes. This will undoubtedly make it easier to look at the finer details, which provide a better clarity of purpose. Scholars of old have made this very clear. In the words of al-Shāṭibi: "Many and numerous may be the issues addressed in a surah. It remains, nevertheless, a single whole linking its beginning with its end, having an overall objective to which all its parts relate in the same way as sentences expressing a single idea are interrelated. Anyone who wishes to study the structure of a surah must begin by looking at it as a single whole, just as they must look at the whole idea before considering its details."

This shows how mistaken students of the Qur'an are when they look at the detailed links between two or more adjacent issues, without considering the overall system that applies to the whole surah. Such a partial look will only deflect a person off his purpose. It will screen from him the most beautiful aspects of the construction. Such a person is like one who is shown a piece of fine and elaborate embroidery to admire, but he decides to look at its threads and details, one at a time, without lifting his eyes once to cast an overall look at the whole piece. He finds a white thread next to a black one, joining other threads of widely different colours without appropriate matching or contrast. Thus, he concludes that it is defective. Had he stretched his sight further to contemplate its design and the picture it gives, he would have noticed coherence between its constituent parts that would elude him when looking only at single elements. He will realise that each colour in each group relates to, or contrasts with, another in a different group. If he then looks at the garment as a whole, taking into view its outer and middle parts,

10 The Unity of Each *Surah*

he will appreciate the harmony and elaborate design that has gone into it. He will then begin to appreciate its exceptional beauty.

This is, indeed, how we should look at the Qur'an if we want to appreciate the order of arrangement each surah follows.

The Wrong Way to Look for Harmony

Before we embark on our study of the longest surah of the Qur'an as an example of the perfect unity of each surah, we need to say a word to anyone who wishes to study the construction of the Qur'an.

When one contemplates the harmony between different parts of the surah, it is vitally important to realise that the relevance of one part to another is not confined to their having some similar or identical aspects, or there being some other physical similarities between them. Some of those who have based their work on such a premise were forced to make some arbitrary claims to prove such links. Others went in the opposite direction and, whenever they found no such similarities, claimed an abrupt break in the flow of the text. Such breaks are not uncommon in old Arabic styles. Indeed, some of them have claimed that the Qur'an uses the method of abrupt breaks as an essential feature of its style.

This method of limiting the study of relevance to the adjacent parts only, and going further to insist on semantic relevance, puts the whole exercise into a straight jacket. Hence, it has led either to arbitrary claims that one seeks to impose without justification, or to a denial of relevance. Hence, it is a highly hazardous method of investigation to apply to the Qur'an. It betrays a total lack of appreciation of the superior quality of the Qur'anic style and its exceptional merits.

If we were to try to erase the naturally distinctive features of the different meanings and purposes the Qur'an expresses in a single surah, we deprive the Qur'an of one of its most essential qualities. This is the fact that the

Qur'an never labours an issue at such a length as to make it boring. Indeed, the Qur'an is never boring when we give it our full attention.

On the other hand, if, for the sake of preserving the integrity of such meanings and purposes, we try to put them apart and remove their semantic and structural relevance to each other, we will deprive the Qur'an of another essential quality. That is, it never changes subject abruptly, without preparing the listener for the forthcoming conclusion of one subject and the beginning of another. Indeed the Qur'an has a most solid and interlinked structure.

What is important to realise is that when the Qur'an groups together divergent types, it moulds them in such a way that they appear to make a coherent picture. In fact it makes their apparent difference the basis of their grouping. This sort of moulding of widely different elements in a single whole is the crux of excellence in every artistic endeavour. It is the standard which measures degrees of creativity and taste in fine art. Maintaining harmony and coherence between several divergent elements and unrelated colours is a much harder pursuit than trying to achieve that between various shades or aspects of the same colour or element.

Following this rule, the Qur'an sometimes places opposites next to each other in order to most clearly highlight their contrasting characteristics. At other times, it groups together matters that are different, though not opposite, so that they give each other mutual emphasis, perhaps through contrast, sub-division, citing examples, deduction, complement or exception, etc. It may make use of a feature of an event or a place, which is common to two purposes, in order to support grouping them together in the structure of the surah. A person who is oblivious to these aspects may view the linking of the two purposes to be unnatural. It, however, is not. It responds to the needs of the listener who feels the link between the two purposes. If the two meanings or purposes have no natural link between them, the Qur'an would then move from one to the other very gently, either easing its way through, or using the sort of syntax that allows compatibility between unfamiliar elements.

The Unity of Each *Surah*

We may come across some subtle elements that we admire, but we would not be able to describe these if we were to be asked to pinpoint what gives them their excellence. Indeed, we may find it difficult to determine where exactly the seamless joint occurs. Should we, however, forget about rules and jargon, allow ourselves a free, unrestrained approach, and either read or listen to these passages, we will not feel any abrupt move that may not agree with fine taste or sound odd to the listener. Indeed, we will always feel that there is such beauty of coherence and harmony, even before we are able to determine its cause or how it is achieved.

A discerning reader who is well versed in distinguishing fine style and speech may be able to make such a judgement, on the basis of personal appeal if not on logical deduction, particularly if he still retains a natural sense for Arabic. Should any of us fail to appreciate this overall beauty in any part of the Qur'an, we should only blame ourselves for such failure. We should always remember that the more we appreciate of the excellence of the Qur'an, the better literary sense we have and the more versed we are in language and style. The reverse is also true. When we fail to appreciate the literary merit of a passage of the Qur'an, then our literary sense is suspect. It is sufficient to remember here that the best qualified people to recognise the excellence of the Qur'anic style, Muhammad's own Arab contemporaries, were the ones who acknowledged its superior nature. By way of comparison, we may say that biological scientists may find themselves unable to understand the physiological secrets of some parts of the body. None of them, a believer or a non-believer, could ever say that they serve no beneficial purpose. Indeed, as they thoroughly admire the fine tuning of the whole body and perfect function of its parts, they admit that there remain some secrets as yet unknown to man, but which they hope to uncover one day.

The elements the Qur'an uses in joining diverse passages are all fine tools which provide coherence between one meaning or purpose and another. But the beauty of the Qur'anic structure is not always founded on selecting which particular purpose should follow the preceding one. It may complete tackling one group of meanings before turning to a contrasting group. Placing each group in its assigned place may provide an implicit signal to contrast the first or the last elements in both, or it may be to contrast the first element of one group with the last of the other.

What is most important, then, is to look at the whole structure of the surah, as we have already emphasised. We will now give an example from one surah which will serve as a model for studying all surahs if one wishes to do so.

Chapter 11

The Semantic Design of the Longest *Surah*

Very long as Surah 2, *al-Baqarah* or The Cow, is, it forms a complete whole consisting of an introduction, four purposes and a conclusion, as follows:

The Introduction defines the Qur'an, [which in this instance may be taken to mean the whole of the book or this particular surah]. It makes clear that the guidance it provides has been made so obvious that only a person who suffers from sickness in his heart, or who is without a heart, will hesitate to accept it.

The first purpose is a call addressed to all mankind to accept Islam and to believe in it.

The second purpose makes a special appeal to the people of earlier Divine religions to abandon the falsehood they introduced into their religions and to embrace the true faith.

The third purpose is an extensive and detailed presentation of the laws of this faith.

The fourth purpose mentions the religious nature that guides people to adhere to these laws and to refrain from violating them.

The conclusion defines those who have responded to this general call and outlines what reward they may expect in this life and in the life to come.

We will now begin our discussion of how the *surah* tackles each one of its purposes throughout its text running into 286 verses, some of which are very long.

The Introduction: (Verses 1-20)

1. The surah begins with three separate letters, *alif, lām, mīm* (corresponding to 'A, L, M'). The Arabs at the time never placed such letters at the beginning of their poetry or prose. They are normally used by teachers beginning their instruction of young children by teaching them the alphabet. Whatever the purpose these letters are intended to serve, stating them at the outset is bound to attract attention and alert listeners to this unfamiliar style.

2. Three phrases then follow, the first of which announces to the listener that what is going to be recited now is the best book ever produced. Indeed, nothing in the whole universe may be described as a book, when compared to this one: *"This is the Book."*

The other two phrases support this verdict with solid evidence. Indeed, the value of any book is in the truth it contains, and in portraying such truth in a bright light so that no doubt or confusion is raised about it. The perfection of such value, then, lies in the great need people have to understand that truth in order to see their way clearly. It should provide them with indisputable proof of its guidance should they find themselves at a loss, unable to determine which way to follow. This being so, the Qur'an combines all these three values: it is the pure truth that admits no trace of falsehood, providing clear guidance that takes mankind out of darkness into light: *"This is the Book, no doubt: a guidance."* (2: 2.)

These are the three phrases that follow the three initial letters with which the surah starts. They alert us to the subject matter and then begin to highlight its virtues. It is the method followed by a good educator: he begins by drawing the attentions of his listeners, then employs the tools that make them eager to know more.

3. The first thing we want to know after this telling description of the Qur'an and the guidance it provides is to know what effect it will have on people as also their response to its call. This clearly means that, with respect to their attitude towards this book, people will always fall into one of three groups: those that believe in it, those that reject it, and those who remain unsure, hesitant, joining neither of the other two.

Now how does the surah turn its attention from talking about the book so as to speak about people? Does it make a new beginning, or treat it as an appendix to what has been said? It does neither, but mixes the two purposes in a most subtle way that may escape the attention of even the most alert of readers. At first, it does not mention the last two groups, as though the Qur'an is not addressed to them at all. It only speaks of the first group, making its reference to it as part of its description of the Qur'an as providing guidance. It says of the Qur'an: "*A guidance for the God-fearing who believe...*". (2: 2-3.) This means that the preposition, '*for*', serves as a secret passage directing the discourse so as to attend fully to the believers whose qualities are now outlined.

4. Limiting the benefit of Qur'anic guidance to this group only, after having described the Qur'an as the clear truth which is subject to no doubt whatsoever, sounds amazing to the listener. How is it possible that the Qur'anic truth should be so clear, but cannot find its way into the heart of every listener?

On the other hand, the Prophet Muhammad, compassionate as he was, was keen that his community should follow the guidance of the Qur'an and believe in God. He might have thought that his hopes would be fulfilled once he had taken the right steps towards it, and that his people would surely become Muslims once they listened to the Qur'an. Yet the Qur'an almost defines its own task, stating that only the God-fearing will benefit by its guidance. Perhaps the Prophet might have appealed to his Lord, saying: All glory is Yours! But why does its guidance not benefit all mankind?

It is necessary, then, to state the facts very clearly so as to put an end to any unrealistic hopes, so that one does not try to pursue what is impossible. The reasons that prevent the Qur'anic guidance from benefiting all people must be stated clearly in a way that shows that the fault does not lie with the Qur'an but rather with its recipients. It is no reflection on the ability of a doctor that his patient dies as a result of failing to take the medicine he has prescribed. Nor does it detract from the value of the sun that those who are blind cannot see its light. *"As for the unbelievers, it is alike whether you forewarn them or not, they will not accept the faith."* (2: 6.)

Thus, the *surah* proceeds to speak about the unbelievers who deserve God's punishment after it has completed its outline of the characteristics of the believers who merit God's reward. Discussion of the two groups is not shown to be intended initially: this would have meant that a conjunction should be used. But progress of the discussion from one group to the other appears to come so naturally in order to answer the unspoken question and to remove the listener's amazement.

5. The discussion of the unbelievers runs to its fullness, with the third group joining the second, as they both reject the Qur'anic guidance. At heart, they are the same, although they may speak differently: *"There are some who say: 'We believe in God and the Last Day,' yet they are not true believers."* (2: 8.)

6. If we now look at the way the surah treats each of the three groups we find that their positions are clearly contrasted. In speaking about each group, the surah discusses three points in the following order: outlining the real situation of each group, pointing out the reasons which determine it and informing us about the expected destiny of each group.

The truth about the first group is that it consists of people who have attained the quality of being God-fearing, in its theoretical and practical senses. They adhere to God's guidance and their Lord supports them. Hence, this group will achieve the success to which they aspire.

The truth of the second group is that they are devoid of fearing God, that is, they are devoid of faith. Not only this, but they are so hardened in their attitude that no warning is of any use to them. The reason being that they do not make use of the faculties of understanding and knowledge God has given them. They have minds but they do not understand; they have eyes but they do not see; and they have ears but they do not hear. Hence, they deserve their inevitable destiny of suffering grievous punishment.

The truth of the third group is a composite of good appearance and an evil reality. They profess to be believers, but they are totally devoid of faith. Each aspect of their condition has a reason and an outcome. Their claim to believe results from their deliberate intention to deceive. The outcome of such deception is that they are the ones who are deceived. That they harbour disbelief is due to the fact that they are sick at heart. The result is that their sickness of heart is aggravated and that they will be made to suffer painful punishment.

Just like the surah has shown that the second group has reached a level of obstinacy and stupidity that renders any warning useless, the third group is shown to have reached a level of ignorance and arrogance which makes any advice given to them futile. They claim to be rational and to do nothing but good, when really they are but fools, spreading corruption. How is it possible to cure a diseased person when he believes himself to be in good health? Then just as the surah records that the first group follows right guidance and will surely prosper, it records that the other two groups are in error and that they will be the losers.

7. This truthful description of the two groups [i.e. the second and the third] does not quench our amazement at their positions. It is normally the case that people differ on ambiguous and confusing matters, not on the clear truth. That these people take a wrong position towards the Qur'an when it sets out the truth that bears no doubt is strikingly odd. Hence, it needs a practical example that brings it closer to our minds, so that we are certain that it happens in reality. The surah gives an example of each of these two groups.

Perfect Unity of Whole and Part

Those who are hardened in their disbelief and whose hearts are sealed are likened to a group of people travelling by night in total darkness. One of them had the foresight to light up a fire to provide them with some light. But when the fire had illuminated the surrounding area, some of them refused to open their eyes to the light. Instead, something happened to deprive them of their eyesight. All their faculties were rendered useless as a result. This example is akin to the light brought into the life of the Arabs, an unlettered nation, by Muhammad[9] (peace be upon him) after a long period of time in which no prophet had come to any community. This light illuminated those hearts that opened up to receive it. However, those who persisted in their erring ways, arrogantly preferring to live in the darkness of ignorance, have not opened their eyes to the new light. Instead, they adopted the attitude of one who is deaf and blind. "*Say: To the believers, this Qur'an is a guidance and a source of health; but as for those who will not believe – they have deafness in their ears, and to them, it is a [cause of] blindness.*" (41: 44.)

The hypocrites who were bent on deception are likened to a community of people on a night of thunderstorms and torrential rain. They leave the

---

9   This example occurs in verse 17 which may be rendered as follows: "*They are like one who sought to kindle a fire, and as it is lit up all around him God took away their light and left them in darkness, unable to see anything. Deaf, dumb and blind, they can never return to the right path.*" All commentaries on the Qur'an we have seen interpret the person kindling the fire as a reference to the hypocrites. This made the author very reluctant to suggest that it refers to the Prophet Muhammad (peace be upon him), without first having some evidence in support of such a view. It took a long time before we found the evidence in a hadith quoting the Prophet as saying: "To give an example of myself and all people: I am just like one who sought to kindle a fire, and as it lit up all around him, butterflies and crawling insects started racing into it. He tries to prevent them and they overpower him and go straight into it. I am trying hard to hold you away from the fire and you persist in trying to reach it." [Related by al-Bukhari and Muslim.] It is true the likeness given here is different from that in the Qur'anic verse, but that does not matter. The same example may be given for different purposes. What is important for us here is that the person in the simile is the Prophet himself. This gave us the reassurance that our understanding was appropriate.

rain water to be wasted, making no use of it for their drinking needs, or for irrigation, or for their cattle. They give their full attention to the lightning, thunder and the total darkness of the night. Time after time, they wait for the lightning so that they may walk, then when it is over and the darkness overwhelms them again, they stand still, waiting for the next lightning so that they may continue to walk.

This example refers to the Qur'an, which gives life to people's hearts in the same way as rain brings forth life from the earth. Its fruits are seen in good deeds, fine manners and a proper sense of morality. It sets for the believers the test of jihad, patience in adversity and endurance of hardship, in peace or war, victory or defeat. Some people profess to accept it, but do not truly believe in it. They do not experience the fulfilment it gives to their hearts and souls. They only look at it from the narrow angle of what they stand to make of gain or loss. They are prepared to change their attitude to it on the basis of personal interest. If they expect an easy gain to come out of a comfortable trip, they will follow the lure of expected riches. Thus, they are quick to join the believers. When war breaks out and the risks of death or defeat loom large, however, they do not hesitate to desert, giving any excuse they think to be plausible. They may even turn back after marching part of the way with the believers, declaring that they do not think there will be any fighting.

If the situation before them is blurred, neither offering prospects of gain nor raising risks of loss, they will stick to the middle ground, making no real commitment. They will wait for the result so that they may side with the winner: *"If triumph comes to you from God, they say, 'Were we not on your side?' – whereas if the unbelievers are in luck, they say to them, 'Have we not earned your affection by defending you against the believers?'"* (4: 141.) *"There are among you such as would lag behind, and then, if calamity befalls you, say, 'God has bestowed His favour on me in that I was not present with them!' But if good fortune comes to you from God, such a person is sure to say – just as if there had never been any question of love between you and him – 'Would that I had been with them so that I might have a share in their great success.'"* (4: 72-73.)

This is the typical attitude of the hypocrites in all situations. Whenever they expect an easy gain, they will go after it wherever it happens to be. If they expect harm or loss, they will turn away. They will sacrifice nothing for any cause. When the prospects are unclear, they stand in the middle, making no commitment. In this they are totally different from the believers who choose to follow the truth, ready to sacrifice for it whatever they are called upon to sacrifice.

Thus, the introduction is completed, having given the right description of the Qur'an, and having truthfully described those who follow it and those who deny its truth. The description of all three groups, as they choose their attitudes towards the Qur'an, will undoubtedly emphasise the status of the Qur'an. As its followers are described as following right guidance and as sure to prosper, while those who deny it are followers of error who will end up in ruin, then there is no doubt that the Qur'an embodies the truth.

What is this truth followed only by rightly guided people who are certain to prosper and denied only by the losers? Indeed, what is this truth that is here likened to bright light and abundant rain? Such descriptions serve to enhance people's interest to learn what the Qur'an preaches. The surah now outlines the main beliefs of Islam. Here we have a very interesting feature of style. So far, the surah has spoken about the Qur'an and the three groups of people using the third person mode. In ordinary style, this would have been maintained in describing Islamic beliefs. However, this mode is now abandoned and the form of address to all mankind is employed. The next verse says: *"Mankind, worship your Lord, who has created you and those who lived before you..."*. (2: 21.) So why does this change occur?

The accurate and precise description of the three groups, believers, unbelievers and hypocrites, has changed their status for the listener. At the beginning, they were absentees, with only their characteristics being delineated. Now that they have been faithfully and accurately described, they are present in the listener's mind, as though he is looking at them in a place where they can be addressed. Hence, it is possible to address them as though they are physically present. On the other hand, the examples given of the unbelievers have given the listener a very sad picture of them indeed. He is eager to give them honest advice and sound warning. He wants to call out to them or to hear someone addressing them to open their eyes and follow the path that ensures their safety. We are, thus, fully prepared for the mode of address when it comes in the next verse: "*Mankind, worship your Lord, who has created you and those who lived before you...*". That is how the surah begins its first purpose which we will discuss presently.

The Main Islamic Beliefs

Remembering that this is the longest surah in the Qur'an, taking no less than 286 verses, we find that the first purpose takes only five verses, 21-25, which send a powerful address to all mankind calling on them to meet three requirements: 1) that they worship none other than God, associating no partners with Him whatsoever; 2) that they should believe in the book He has revealed to His servant and Messenger; and 3) that they should guard against incurring God's painful punishment and should try to earn His plentiful reward.

These three requirements are the basic three principles of the Islamic faith, set out in their natural order: a beginning, a middle and an end. The first two are set out with logical, irrefutable proofs that leave no room for any doubt. The third is given without such proof. It is presented with a powerful appeal to the human conscience, along with much promise and warning to compensate for material proof. Yet when we consider this third principle carefully, we realise that it needs no proof, after the first two have been firmly established. It is, in a way, a logical consequence of these two principles.

Let us take the case of an ambassador delivering a message from a powerful king whose authority is unchallenged. The recipient makes sure that the message is actually sent by the king, bearing his seal. Does he need any further proof of the contents of the message, especially when he knows that the sender says only the truth and always honours the promises he makes? This is the case here when the principle in question requires that we believe in something that is reported to us. The report, however, is based on what has already been established with regard to the truth of prophethood. The progress from the first two principles to the third one is masterly: *"But if you fail, as you will always do, then guard yourselves against the fire…"*. (2: 24.)

Then follows a recap in 14 verses, 26-39. As stated earlier, the surah opens by a general description of the Qur'an as a source of guidance. It is now appropriate to describe the method of guidance employed in the Qur'an. We learn that it is perfect guidance, setting matters clearly with no ambiguity over any detail. Let us now consider how the recap begins after a progressive transition stretching from the beginning of the surah.

In the introduction, the three classes of people are described fully, with examples setting out their respective attitudes and conditions. It states very clearly that the unbelievers have chosen to follow falsehood, while the believers follow the truth they receive from their Lord. In outlining the first purpose, the surah makes it clear that God is unlike anything. No equals may be set up for Him, and no partners may be associated with Him. This is followed by establishing a criterion to distinguish a true prophet sent with God's message from one who makes a false claim to prophethood. This criterion takes the form of a universal challenge that stands for all time, a challenge to produce a single surah like the Qur'an. This is followed by examples describing the fire of hell which is prepared for the unbelievers, and heaven which is promised to the God-fearing.

In all these examples the Qur'an refers to a wide variety of facts, some are sublime while others mundane, some material and some spiritual. This culminates with a presentation of the comforts and pleasures enjoyed in heaven, including some that are personal or even carnal. Indeed, some people may feel shy when they are mentioned, while an uneducated person may think that a discourse by God would not refer to such things. Such a thought may be entertained only when a person overlooks the fact that God is the Truth who does not hesitate to state the facts, and that He is the Merciful who bestows His grace on mankind, telling them all that they need to know in the language they understand. He explains to them in plain terms all issues concerning what they may love or hate, hope for or fear.

Having given all these examples, the surah deduces from them a general rule that sets out the Qur'anic method in providing guidance. It gives all sorts of examples and sets out all facts, pleasant or bitter, putting everything in its right place, calling it by its plain name. It does not refrain from referring to any matters, large or small, great or mundane: "*It would not be beneath God to give the parable of a gnat, or a higher creature.*" (2: 26.) It is, indeed, the case that this book outlines in plain terms what is true and what is false, what is beneficial and what is harmful, omitting nothing, just like the record each one of us will have on the Day of Judgement showing all our good deeds and all our bad ones.

People's Attitudes towards the Qur'an

The general description of the Qur'an at the outset as a book of guidance has led to mentioning people's attitudes to that guidance, and to a denunciation of those who reject its guidance. A similar distinction results here from mentioning the Qur'anic method of providing guidance: "*By it He leaves many to stray and many He enlightens and guides.*" (2: 26.) Again, those who choose to go astray are denounced here with an outline of their evil deeds: "*He, however, will leave to stray none but the evil-doers.*" (2: 26.) The description of the unbelievers in the introduction provides an image that makes us eager to listen to the address calling on them to pay heed and accept God's message. Their qualities described here make us eager to listen to how they are rebuked for their denial of the truth: "*How can you reject God when He has given you life after you were dead? He will cause you to die again then He will bring you back to life. To Him you shall surely return. It is He who has created for you all that is on earth. He then turned to heaven and fashioned it into seven heavens. He has knowledge of all things."* (2: 28-29.)

We are now back to the first purpose with all its three principles, but these are put here in a different format. As for the first principle, it is made initially in the form of an order to worship God. Here, the order is not to disbelieve in God. In the first instance, the surah reminds them in general terms of the blessing of their creation. Here, the reminder comes in full detail. They are told at the beginning that both the heavens and earth are made to sustain their life. Now they are told about this in more detail.

With regard to the second principle, the prophethood of Muhammad, God's last Messenger, is mentioned first, but now the surah mentions the prophethood of the first of all prophets, Adam. This tells us that Muhammad is not a new phenomenon represented in a man given a message by God. Indeed, the concept of prophethood and Divine legislation is as old as the beginning of human life on earth. This is well prepared by making mention of man's remarkable origin and then by its discussion with the angels. This discussion, as reported in the surah, proves the extra care God has given to mankind who have been chosen to be in charge of building life on earth and who have been given the superior quality of knowledge that distinguishes them from other creatures. That God has bestowed His grace on man and given him all these blessings ties up with the outline of God's other favours given earlier in respect of the first principle. The favours God has given to man were the cause of Satan's envy of man and hostility towards Adam, the first man created. This led to Satan's wicked deception culminating in both of them being subjected to a trial. Both are given a mission to fulfil. The progress of the discussion is natural, with all its points developing easily and naturally.

As for the third principle we see that in the first instance both heaven and hell are given an awesome description. Here, they are mentioned only by name and by indicating the dwellers of each of them. Reward and duty are mentioned side by side to indicate that the one leads to the other. What this means is that the fulfilment of duty leads to happiness in the Hereafter, while neglecting it leads to misery.

Here again the recap ends with a reference to the unbelievers in order to address some of them and to call on them to believe in Islam, which is the second purpose of the surah, treated in 123 verses (40-162). It should be remembered that this surah was the first to be revealed in Madinah, where the most hostile enemies of Islam lived. These were the Jews, the most argumentative about faith, as they relied on the knowledge vouchsafed to them through God's earlier messengers. This shows us the keen attention given to calling on them particularly to believe in the new faith, after the call addressed to all mankind. It tells us why they are addressed in a friendly manner at times, and why the Qur'an talks about them at other times in different styles, ranging from the offensive to the defensive, and from trying to win them over to putting the facts clear before them. This takes us beyond the middle point of this longest surah. As we read through, moving from one stage to another, we are overawed with the structure and accurate design of the surah.

The address to the Jews begins with a single short verse that sums up all that the Qur'an needs to say to them: *"Children of Israel, remember My favours which I have bestowed on you. Fulfil your covenant with Me and I will fulfil My covenant with you; and of Me alone stand in awe."* (2: 40.) It addresses them by the name they love most, reminding them of their relationship to Jacob and Abraham, as well as of the totality of the favours God has bestowed on them. This forms the basis for the call to them to fulfil their pledges, adding promises of reward and threats of punishment. It then begins to explain all this in more detail, starting with an outline in six verses, 41-46, of the covenant which they are required to fulfil. Verse 47 describes the extent of God's favours which they are required to remember, while verse 48 details the extent of God's warning to them.

Address to the Jews

The subsequent discussion is divided into four sections: 1) an account of the history of the Jews ever since Moses was sent with God's message to them; 2) an exposition of the conditions of those Jews living at the time of the revelation of Islam, Muhammad's message; 3) a discussion of the higher position of the Muslims ever since the time of Abraham; and 4) an exposition of the situation of the Muslims at the time of the Prophet Muhammad. We will discuss these four themes as tackled in the *surah*.

1. The History of the Jews (Verses 49-74)

This section begins with eight verses in which God reminds the Israelites of the blessings which God had bestowed on them time after time, giving them much of their details. These were the historical blessings which lasted for a long time and benefited one generation of Jews after another. It reminds them of the great occasions when God first saved them from Pharaoh and his people, and then saved them from drowning in the sea, while leaving their enemies to be so engulfed. Then they have a reminder of God's promise to bestow His revelations on them, and the fact that He had fulfilled that promise and sent down revelations for their guidance. A further reminder mentions the fact that God accepted their repentance after they had reverted back to associating partners with Him, and then again He accepted their repentance when they had rebelled against their Prophet and put to him great demands. All these were great favours bestowed on them 'before and after their commitment of sin'. Mentioning them should soften their hearts and motivate them to acknowledge God's favours and express gratitude to Him and to obey His orders.

After this reminder of former favours, which are plentiful and wide ranging, another reminder of a different kind is intended, but this time it mentions their offences and the punishment they suffered for them. However, the surah separates the two reminders with a short passage in which it mentions some of God's favours and their response to them. We are first prepared for this intervening passage by a brief note that mentions their turning away showing displeasure. Here, we are told that God has given them on top of all those favours some special blessings such as sending clouds to comfort them with shade and giving them food and drink which they received without having to work for them. Nevertheless, they wronged themselves, looked at those blessings with contempt, distorted their expression of gratitude to make it an expression of ridicule, and asked for a life of toil to replace their life of comfort. God has committed them to what they suggested and has imposed on them a life of ignominy and humiliation.

Mention of their offences and the punishment they were made to suffer for them follows this intervening passage. The surah mentions that they earned the burden of God's condemnation because of their disbelief in the signs given to them by God and because they killed prophets, making an exception only in the case of those of them who adhered to the faith. They further disobeyed God's orders outlined in the Torah until they were forced to heed them. However, they subsequently disregarded these orders to the extent that they earned God's displeasure and deserved the punishment that befell those who sinned against the Sabbath, but God bestowed His grace on them nevertheless. They were also slack to carry out the orders of their prophet. They were so naïve in their understanding of prophethood that they thought that he was jesting about some of what he conveyed to them.

Verse 74 provides a link between the first two sections. The surah wants to establish a link between their situation in the past and in the period when the Qur'an was revealed. It places this link in the verse with which it concludes the first section: *"Yet after all this your hearts hardened until they have become as hard as rocks or even harder."* The phrase, *'yet after all this'*, indicates the beginning of the hardening of their hearts, without putting a limit to it. This suggests that it was progressive, continuing over generations. The listener is left with the impression that this hardening has continued to the present day. This impression is further emphasised by usage of the present tense in describing the hardness of their hearts: '*until they have become as hard as rocks.*' This is far more expressive than saying, 'until they were as hard as rocks.'

As the verse describes their hearts in this way, it makes this description a reason for a change of address. When a person's heart is so hardened that it becomes like a rock, it is unwise to carry on any further discussion with him. It is, indeed, wiser to turn to someone else whose heart is free of sickness and to speak to him. This is indeed what happens here. The surah stops addressing them about their ancestors and begins speaking to the Muslims about the Jews who were contemporaries of the Prophet and his companions.

2. The Jews in Madinah at the Dawn of Islam (Verses 75-121)

As said earlier, the second purpose of the surah may be divided into 4 sections. The second section, verses 75-121, deals with the situation of the Jews in Madinah at the time of the Prophet Muhammad (peace be upon him). It opens with an unusual sentence that does not follow the reporting style of the previous or subsequent verses. It is an interrogative sentence preceded by one particle and followed by another. The first particle, '*fa*', reminds us of all the incidents mentioned in the first section, while the second, '*wa*', opens the door to all events that are to be mentioned in this section. Between the past and the present history this sentence serves to indicate the lesson to be learnt. The reasons leading to past events and those ushering in future ones make the result a foregone conclusion: "*Do you, then, hope that they will accept your message when some of them....*" (2: 75.)

The first particle, *fa*, which is given in translation as, '*then*', serves to say to us: 'Is it conceivable after all that has been told that anyone could hope that such people, heirs to all this unsavoury history, could accept the faith?' The second particle, *wa*, which is translated here as, '*when*', tells us: 'Not only so, but they have committed even worse deeds and these they continue to perpetrate.'

After this short sentence, the surah reverts back to the reporting style, mentioning various deeds and sayings done or said by these contemporary Jews, giving in the process around 20 reasons that leave absolutely no hope that they will ever accept the faith honestly. Some of these reasons apply to them alone, while some are common to others as well, such as their own ancestors, as also to Christians and idolaters. As the surah mentions a claim or allegation made by the Jews, it adds a clear reply to refute it.

This description of the conditions of these contemporary Jews divides them at the outset into two groups: scholars who deliberately distort God's words, urging one another to conceal their knowledge so that it is not taken as an argument against them. The other group includes ignorant, unlettered people who pursue their hopes and superstitions. These are victims of the distortion perpetrated by their rabbis. In such a situation, who could entertain any hope in the reformation of a community in which the masses are deceived into adding to their religion what does not belong to it, while its scholars deliberately deceive people into accepting as Divine revelation what they themselves have invented.

This is followed by providing the origin of their shameless attitude making it easy for them to commit every kind of sin. This is due to their arrogance which led them to claim that they would not be tortured in hell except perhaps for a few days. The Prophet is ordered to refute this claim in unequivocal language. He is instructed to put his argument in a progressive way, beginning by pursuing a rational and logical approach starting with a request that they should produce evidence in support of their claims. It then refutes their claim showing that it is at variance with the basic elements of the law of Divine justice which admits no favouritism or injustice whatsoever. All human beings are equal before this law, with everyone held responsible for their deeds. Whoever does good or evil will have just reward for it.

Then the surah turns the scales against them, showing clearly that they belong to the camp of people who '*earn evil and become engulfed by their sins*' (2: 82). Have they not made a covenant committing themselves to remain

God-fearing and to do good to other people, but have failed to honour their covenant? Have they not pledged to refrain from sin and injustice, yet they are immersed in injustice? On top of this they believe in certain portions of God's book and deny others. They also make God's law subject to their desires. Whenever a messenger comes to them with something that is in conflict with their wishes, they turn away in arrogance.

This is followed by a full list of their other misdeeds: a long list indeed that may be summed up as follows:

1. Their refusal to listen to the message of the truth, justifying their attitude by claiming that their hearts are sealed;

2. Their rejection of the new Divine book only because it has been revealed to a person who does not belong to them. Yet they were awaiting the new message, hoping to follow the new prophet so that they would be able to overcome the pagan Arabs;

3. Their claims of fulfilling their duty by believing in what was revealed to them. The fact is that they disbelieve even in their own revelations. They have continued to make these claims ever since they worshipped the calf and loved that sort of worship;

4. Their claims that ultimate success in the Hereafter will be theirs alone. Yet they contradict their very claims by their fear of death and by their desire to prolong their life in this world as much as possible;

5. Their hostility to Gabriel, the angel, because he delivered God's revelations to someone who did not belong to them. The fact is that the revelation is made under God's instructions and in His knowledge;

6. Their repeated violations of their covenants;

7. Their preoccupation with learning books of black magic, while discarding God's book;

8. Twisting their tongues when speaking to the Prophet, pronouncing a certain word, *rā'ina*, in a way that made it a word of ridicule directed at him and his faith, although they professed to use it as a word of respect. This manipulation and deliberate obscuring of their language sometimes aimed to embarrass the Prophet, putting to him a long list of requests and suggestions, just like they did with Moses. [It should be mentioned here that this point is given in the surah in the form of a warning to the believers not to say that word the Jews used for ridicule.]

9. Their grudges, along with those of other disbelievers among the people of earlier faiths and the polytheists, emanated from their envy that revelation had been vouchsafed to someone else. It is, indeed, up to God to assign prophethood to anyone He chooses. It is, indeed, His prerogative to abrogate any code of law, substituting for it a similar or a better one, as He pleases;

10. The desire entertained by many of them to turn the believers back into disbelief;

11. The claims reiterated by the Jews and the Christians that none other than they will ever be in heaven. Such claims are no more than vain desires that have no solid basis;

12. The mutual claims made by both the Jews and Christians that the other religion has no basis to stand on, while the pagan Arabs said the same thing about both of them;

13. All three groups were keen to forbid the mentioning of God's name in His houses of worship;

14. Their participation in making false claims against God and alleging that He has a son;

15. Their refusal to believe in God's Messengers until God had spoken to them directly, without a medium, or until He had sent them a clear sign.

16. The last of their misdeeds mentioned in the surah is the one leading to total despair on the believers' part that they would ever believe. Indeed, those Jews hoped to convert God's Messenger himself so that he would follow their desires. How, then, could he hope that they would ever believe in the guidance he brought? This is impossible. It is sufficient for him then that those of them who have true knowledge and who read God's book as it should be read believe in his guidance. After all, those who disbelieve are themselves the losers.

3. An Account of Believers Since Abraham (Verses 122-134)

A wise reformer's approach in his advocacy is the same as a farmer who prepares the land for a new season. The latter begins by weeding and clearing the land of dead plants before putting in the new seeds or planting new trees. The same is done by a wise advocate of faith. He begins with preparing the mind and the soul by purging them of all false beliefs and corruption before directing them to the truth and Divine guidance. It is a two-stage approach: clearance and preparation in the first stage and completion of the mission in the second. So far the address to the Children of Israel in the surah has been confined to showing the crookedness of the way they have been following. Indeed, the surah has illustrated this crookedness fully to complete the first stage. Now the second stage begins, showing them the way they should follow.

We have seen how the discussion in the previous section was concluded with the mention of God's guidance and the knowledge He has vouchsafed to His Messenger (peace be upon him). This is coupled with the mention of the group that is most likely to believe in it from among the followers of earlier religions. These are the ones who read God's revelations as they should be read. This conclusion serves as a prelude which prepares us for the new beginning.

The discourse so far in the present theme or purpose of the *surah* has been divided into two sections: one devoted to discussing the situation of the

Israelites in the past and the other to outlining their situation at the time of the Prophet (peace be upon him). It is most fitting, then, to provide a perfect contrast and to speak now about the believers dividing the discussion first to an exposition of their past and then to outlining their present situation.

This is what we will see now. Indeed, we will see an even more perfect contrast, with the discourse taking in the third section the same lines followed in the first, with a direct address to the Israelites. In the fourth section, the same line will be followed as in the second, speaking about the Muslims at present. What is more, the two verses which started the discussion in the first part are used again to start the discussion now. Again, they are invited here to believe in the truth in the same way as they are called upon to turn away from falsehood. This repetition makes it clear to the listener that the discourse will follow the same lines as it followed earlier, but on a parallel route and a new outlook based on similarly solid grounds: *"Children of Israel! Remember My favours which I have bestowed on you, and that I have preferred you above all nations. Beware of a day when no soul shall avail another in any way: when no ransom shall be accepted from any of them, nor shall intercession be of any use and they shall be without succour. When his Lord tested Abraham with certain commandments…."* (2: 122-124.)

Thus, the Jews are called upon to follow in the footsteps of their God-fearing ancestors. This does not take the form of a commandment or an urging which would have proved to be of little use in their case. Instead, it comes in the form of a captivating narrative mentioning aspects of Abraham's glorious history and that of his children and grandchildren in the golden age; the one unanimously agreed by all followers of Divine religions and pagan Arabs to be the high pinnacle of their history. The surah quotes them all as making the same statement which Abraham had urged his seed to adopt, and which his offspring continued to teach to their children and grandchildren. This is the statement which declares one's full submission to God, the Lord of all worlds.

In relating Abraham's history and his leadership of mankind, the surah makes a point of mentioning his prayer to God to appoint a leader for mankind from among his own seed, just like he himself was appointed such a leader. As we see Abraham and his son Ishmael working on the construction of the Kaʿbah, the Inviolable House of worship which God has sanctified and made a place of security towards which people turn in their prayer, the surah relates their passionate prayer to God to bring out of their offspring a community that submits itself to God and to raise in that community a Messenger from among themselves to teach and purify them.

All this serves to establish a strong historical bond between the Prophet Muhammad and his followers on the one hand and those two noble Prophets on the other. This is not merely a bond of family descent. It is a bond of unity in faith and principle. The Prophet and his followers are of the offspring of Abraham and Ishmael. Their existence comes in answer to their prayer; their faith is the same as that of Abraham and Ishmael; they turn in Prayer to the same place and offer the same pilgrimage.

At the same time, the surah declares that such honourable descent is withdrawn from the Jews who trace their blood ancestry to Jacob and Abraham, but who turn away from their faith and disobey their express commands. Of what use is family descent when the bond of faith is severed? It is as the Arabic saying goes: "If a person's deeds do not speed him towards his goal, his family descent will not move him any faster." Here the surah declares: *"That nation have passed away. To them shall be credited what they have earned, and to you what you have earned. You shall not be questioned about what they did."* (2: 134.)

4. The Muslims at the Time of the Prophet (Verses 135-162)

This follows in a natural progression from discussing ancestors to discussing descendants, and from making implicit hints to a clear and explicit statement. It begins by stating unequivocally that the present Muslim community has a strong bond with that community of believers, both in the fundamentals of its faith and in its main details. The surah relates the attempts of the weak-minded among the Israelites and other communities to deprive the Muslims of this bond, calling on the Muslims to follow their own direction of prayer and denouncing the change of the direction of Islamic prayer from facing Jerusalem to facing the Ka˙bah. All these attempts are shown to be false and of little consequence.

We have seen how the surah has earlier combined its account of Abraham's faith with speaking about the direction he faced in his prayers. This provides a solid basis here to speak about the Islamic faith and its direction of prayer.

As for the faith itself, the surah reminds the Muslims that they are faced with calls from Jews and Christians to follow their creeds. The Muslims are instructed to reply that they will follow the pure faith of Abraham, based on total submission to God. They are to make clear to them that this pure faith requires a complete belief in God and in all that has been revealed to all prophets. We make no distinction between them. To which of these two parts of our faith do you object? Is it to our belief in God, who is our Lord and your Lord? Or is it to following Abraham and his offspring who were neither Jews nor Christians: *"That nation have passed away. To them shall be credited what they have earned, and to you what you have earned. You shall not be questioned about what they did."* (2: 141.)

This should have been sufficient to put an end to all their arguments and to close this door in their faces. It makes it clear that the basic principles of faith are too strong to admit any argument of any sort. The surah moves on quickly to refute their other argument concerning the Ka˙bah, which is the centre of two of the most important acts of worship in Islam, namely, prayer and pilgrimage. The position of the Ka˙bah in the Divine faith had already been established when Abraham and Ishmael made it a place of sanctity and turned towards it in prayer. But this was not sufficient to silence those who were bent on criticising the Muslims for the change of their direction in prayer from Jerusalem to the Ka˙bah. Those evil-minded people used such a change to raise doubts concerning the Prophet's message. Their criticism affected the weaker elements of the Muslim community. Hence, it was necessary to make a strong argument here to refute all the fallacies those hostile elements used to spread.

We see here how the surah directs much of its attention to this issue. It begins by instructing the Prophet to answer those who questioned the wisdom behind the change in a dignified manner, stating that this is a matter decided by the One who may not be questioned about His orders or deeds. The Prophet is told to say to them: all directions are the same, and God directs us to face whichever one He chooses. It is He who guides to the straight path. It follows this with instructions addressed either to the Prophet, in person, or to the believers, and at times to both the Prophet and the believers. All these instructions state emphatically and in detail that the Muslims must maintain their direction of Prayer all the time, wherever they happen to be, in their places of residence or to whichever place they may travel.

The surah intersperses these confirmed commandments with various aspects of old and new Divine legislation. It makes clear that the choice of the temporary direction of prayers was no more than a test of the strength of faith among those believers who migrated from Makkah. The test proves who would sincerely and resolutely follow the Prophet and who would turn back on their heels.

The choice of the new, permanent direction for prayer has a number of reasons and important objectives behind it. It is the middle *qiblah*, i.e. direction of prayer, which is most suitable for the middle community, i.e. the Muslims; and it is the one which meets the desire of the Prophet who turned his face up to heaven, hoping to receive instructions to turn to it without actually putting his wishes into words. It is the *qiblah* which the followers of earlier revelations know to be the true direction determined by their Lord, despite the fact that they concealed it out of envy and arrogance. Moreover, it is the *qiblah* which God testifies to be the true way, and it is the one which leaves no argument for any fair-minded person. As for those who are unfair, they will continue to argue about it as long as they remain hostile to you. Hence, do not fear them. Prepare yourselves, instead, to make whatever sacrifice you are called upon to make for God's cause. Remain patient in adversity and do not grieve for those of you who will be killed in defending God's cause, because such death represents permanent life.

The surah then indicates that continued argument about the *qiblah* not only represents an act of turning people away from the acts of worship done inside the Sacred Mosque. It is also an aggression aimed at turning people away from other acts of worship done near it: "*Al-Safa and al-Marwah are among the symbols set up by God.*" (2: 159.) It explains the true nature of these symbols in the same way as it explained the nature of the *qiblah*, denouncing the people of earlier revelations who were fully aware of their origins in Abraham's history, but who nevertheless knowingly concealed the truth God had revealed.

Strengthening Believers' Resolve

Thus, the four sections in this second purpose or theme of the *surah*, which calls on the Israelites to believe in Islam, are completed. We have seen how the surah arranges them and follows that arrangement step by step. If we now look very carefully at this last section, we realise that the Qur'an makes use of its position to achieve two distinct objectives. Thus, it serves as a bridge between two purposes that are widely apart. On the whole it is a special address from God to the Prophet and the believers concerning some private matters of their faith. But this special address is made in two parts, each coloured with the purpose to which it relates. Thus, the two purposes are interlinked in this section.

It starts by telling the believers what their enemies used to say about some Islamic principles. It then clarifies these principles over which those enemies have raised doubts so as to ensure that they continue to shine with the truth. Thus, the beginning signifies the end of those long battles against falsehood. The thrust is then directed to the strengthening of the believers so that they may hold fast to those principles, whether they relate to theoretical or practical matters. They are encouraged in several verses to adhere to those principles. It is, then, most appropriate to make this conclusion a beginning of a new purpose in which the believers are guided to learn the details of Islamic teachings.

This is, indeed, what this special address implies, long as it is and directed slowly towards this new purpose. Anyone who carefully reflects on this can discern within this last section an implicit statement that says: We have now finished fighting with the enemies, and We turn now to Our servants to teach and guide them. We have closed the book that relates to the evildoers and opened the book of the righteous. This last page of address to the Israelites is only the advance battalion of a large army, or indeed the first rays of a dawn of guidance which will usher in the bright new day of faith and replace the black night of falsehood and disbelief. The whole battlefield is now clear of all Israelite ghosts that were covered with the darkness of falsehood when they tried to attack you. You can no longer perceive any of them now or hear even a whisper of them.

Do you see these first rays of the sun of the Islamic law coming to you in the form of general and theoretical principles, to be followed by a host of practical details? The rest of the details will then follow until this sun has reached its zenith in the sky.

Thus, all ears are now open, eager to listen to the details of Islamic legislation. If they are now related in full, we will not feel that such a discussion comes in an abrupt, unprepared way. Yet the Qur'an, following as it does the most accurate of literary criteria which best fulfils people's needs, does not address this purpose immediately without further preparation. It prefers to provide a resting place where the traveller may relax for a while before embarking on a second long trip towards the next goal.

The Creator and the Legislator

The third purpose or theme of the *surah* has a gateway taking up verses 163-177. It is like a corridor stretching from the door of a house to its main building, and it is covered in only three steps: 1) emphasising the oneness of the Creator who deserves to be worshipped; 2) emphasising the oneness of the Commander who must be obeyed; and 3) an index of the commandments and acts of obedience to be fulfilled.

The first step, which asserts the Oneness of God the Creator, is absolutely necessary at this juncture so as to separate what has already been tackled in the surah and what is yet to come. The points just discussed speak about the great importance of the Kaʿbah, Maqām Ibrāhīm, al-Safa and al-Marwah. All this could have given any newcomer to Islam an impression akin to that of paganism and the sanctity it gives to stones and articles, particularly in the vicinity of such places replete with idols and statues. It is necessary, therefore, that the veneration of such places should not be left without proper definition and restriction. The impression to which we have just alluded must also be dispelled. It is especially important to make clear that when worshippers stand at Maqām Ibrāhīm, and when they turn their faces to the Kaʿbah, and when the pilgrims walk between al-Safa and al-Marwah that they do not address their worship to these stones or seek their help, mercy or intercession. They address their worship to God alone, believing that He is the true Lord of all worlds. They carry out His orders and worship Him at the places in which He bestows His grace and blessings in abundance, as He bestowed these on His good servants in the past.

Another purpose is to remind the Muslims of those good servants of God to strengthen the feeling of love in their hearts towards those early believers and to follow in their footsteps. This is certain to link the past history of the nation of believers to its present, so that it is seen as a single nation following the same direction. It turns its face towards the most sublime of goals: "*Your God is the One God: there is no deity save Him.*" (2: 163.) Do you know Him? He is neither the Kaʿbah, nor al-Safa and al-Marwah, nor

The Semantic Design of the Longest *Surah*

Abraham and Maqām Ibrāhīm. He is *"the One God: there is no deity save Him, the Merciful, the Beneficent."* He is the One who embraces all things within His grace and compassion: *"In the creation of the heavens and the earth; in the alternation of night and day; in the ships which sail in the sea with what is useful to man; in the water which God sends down from the sky with which He gives life to the earth after it has been dead, causing all manner of beasts to multiply over it; in the movement of the winds, and in the clouds which run their appointed courses between sky and earth: in all this there are surely signs for people who use their reason."* (2: 164.) He is the One who commands all power, and on the Day of Judgement no one will punish as He punishes. *"If the wrongdoers could but see, as see they will when they receive their punishment, that all power belongs to God and that God's punishment is severe."* (2: 165.)

All this relates to the purpose that the surah has finished with. As for the purpose the surah is about to tackle, this first step is a necessary prelude before beginning to outline practical legislation. It directs our attentions to the source from where we should receive such legislation. When we realise that we have only one Master, and when we submit to Him, we must follow nothing but His orders and acknowledge no legislation but His. A person who acknowledges different deities will be torn apart between those deities with each one of them demanding his share of obedience. He will have too many sources of orders that must be obeyed, such as parents, traditions, social norms, masters and desires. Hence, this first step leads naturally to the second.

The second step emphasises the oneness of the Commander to be obeyed. This is a cornerstone of the Islamic concept of God's oneness. We know that when one believes in God as the only deity, it follows that one must not address any part of one's worship to anyone but the Merciful who creates, provides sustenance, and causes harm and benefit. Similarly, such a belief requires that we assign no share of authority over our actions and behaviour to anyone else. Indeed we must believe that all sovereignty belongs to Him, and that He is the only one who may legislate. Permissible is only what He permits; and forbidden is only what He prohibits. Unbeliever he is who claims that something God has permitted is forbidden, or something He has forbidden is permissible. Just as it is ludicrous that He is acknowledged as the Creator and Sustainer but worship and gratitude are addressed to someone else, it is also ludicrous to acknowledge Him as the Law-giver and turn in obedience to someone else. *"Mankind, eat of what is lawful and wholesome on the earth, and do not follow Satan's footsteps."* (2: 168.)

In emphasising this single authority to legislate the surah takes a similar approach to that in emphasising God's oneness. It begins by making clear to mankind God's abounding grace and unlimited compassion as He has given them an easy code of law that suits their nature. Of the great variety of food available to them, He makes forbidden to them only four types which are foul and evil. He has permitted them to make use of everything else on earth. At times of necessity, all forbidden things become permissible: *"He who is driven to it by necessity, not intending to transgress nor exceeding his need, incurs no sin. God is Much-Forgiving, Merciful."* (2: 173.) Such an approach softens hearts and makes people willing to submit to the orders of their Lord who is very kind to His servants. Who deserves to be obeyed, then: the Lord who makes permissible only the wholesome things and forbids only what is foul, or Satan who *"bids you only to commit evil and indecency and to attribute to God something of which you have no knowledge."* (2: 169.) Who is to be followed: the One who guides to the truth, or those who *"are devoid of all understanding and follow no guidance."* (2: 170.)

This second step emphasising the single authority of legislation makes clear to mankind the extent of God's anger with anyone who conceals His commandments or who changes what He has ordered and what He has forbidden in order to make a paltry gain: *"Those who suppress anything of the Book which God has revealed and barter it away for a small gain shall eat nothing but the fire in their bellies. God will not speak to them on the Day of Judgement, nor will He purify them. A grievous suffering awaits them."* (2: 176.)

When we contemplate the choice of food and earnings to highlight here, rather than any other aspect of permissibility and prohibition, we realise that it represents the firm bond providing complete coherence between what has gone and what is to come of the surah.

From a practical point of view, the subject will soon be discussed in detail. Its mention at this point alerts us to the fact that the new purpose or theme of the surah is soon to begin. With regard to faith, the subject is historically and closely linked to the belief in God's oneness. In the dark ages of ignorance, when pagan people and followers of past revelations began to follow Satan's footsteps and turned away, as a result, from believing in God's oneness, they adopted certain beings whom they claimed to be equal to God and loved them as they would love God. Shortly thereafter, Satan opened the way to them to take partners to God in His legislation after they had adopted partners to God in their worship. They began to forbid what God had made lawful of crops and cattle, and to make lawful what God had forbidden. They even went further than this and invoked at the time of slaughter the names of their false deities. Thus, they combined all three evils: disobedience of God, innovation and polytheism.

It seems that the first aspect of legislation in conflict with God's law was in the field of food and earnings. Hence, the Qur'an makes it a priority after establishing the oneness of God, the Creator and the Sovereign. Hence, you always find it following the establishment of the main principle of faith in God as the only deity in the universe, even in those surahs revealed in Makkah, such as surahs 6, 7, 10 and 16, entitled Cattle, the Heights, Jonah and the Bee, respectively.

An Index of Legislation

The mention made here of people's inventions in respect of permissible and forbidden food and earnings is most fitting, because adding these in the context of God's oneness is parallel to the mention of the rules concerning the direction of prayer in relation to Abraham's faith. Each of these two is an important branch of a major issue. In fact, its discussion here ends in the same way as the discussion of the other topic earlier. Both endings warn those hardened disbelievers "*who conceal what God has sent down.*" Indeed, Islam makes the questions of the direction of prayer and the slaughtering of animals two rituals that give a Muslim his distinctive character, just like he is distinguished by declaring his belief in God's oneness and by his prayer. The Prophet says: "Whoever offers our prayer, turning towards our *qiblah*, and eats our slaughtered animals is a Muslim who qualifies to be party to the covenant with God and His Messenger."

The innovation of prohibition without basis in respect of food and earnings is not limited to those who turn away from the faith. Indeed, some Muslims at the time of the Prophet were close to falling prey to this disease that affected earlier communities. They declared their intention either to refrain from marriage or to prohibit themselves certain types of wholesome food or other things. They did not wish to declare these as forbidden to all people, but rather they looked upon them with contempt. They wanted to force themselves to endure the hardship of abstaining from them, either through a vow or a declaration of will power. The Qur'an stamps out such an innovation and firmly closes the door leading to it so that it does not become a way to forbidding other things. It alerts them to the fact that part of their belief in God's oneness is to adhere to what He has permitted them as an expression of their gratitude to Him, in the same way as they adhere to what He has forbidden them as an expression of their patience: "*Believers, eat of the good things which We have provided for you, and give thanks to God, if it is truly Him that you worship.*" (2: 171.)

Consider now how the address to mankind concerning this very basic principle and what it entails serves as a prelude to addressing the believers specially and outlining the rules applicable to them. This is parallel to the address given first to all mankind at the beginning of the surah outlining the main principles of the Islamic faith and then to the Israelites in particular, calling on them to accept the new faith without hesitation. Could there be any more harmony and symmetry in this address?

Now, that the listener is fully prepared to receive the commandments detailing God's orders and prohibitions, let us consider how the surah makes the third and final step. The third step provides a general index of legislation. Here again we see remarkable aspects of structure and the following of a clear, progressive line.

Consider first the refined link between the previous purpose and the new one. The two are linked verbally, but are separate with regard to their respective positions. When it relates the two verbally, the surah puts us with one foot at the end of the previous purpose and the other at the beginning of the ensuing one. However, it separates them with two particles: one denoting a negative and the other a statement. Thus, it plants both our feet together so that we may move forward. *"Righteousness is not that you turn your faces to the east or the west; but truly righteous is he…."* (2: 177.) This verse tells us that the definition of places and directions in rituals of worship, which was a preoccupation of proponents and opponents alike, is not all that righteousness is concerned with. It is merely a single branch of just one of its many aspects. Righteousness is, indeed, a word that combines all aspects of goodness, theoretical and practical, relating to the treatment of people, to worship of the Creator and to a lofty morality. It is with all these that true believers should be preoccupied.

Consider also how when the surah begins to detail these aspects, it does not relate them all, in full, at the same time. Rather, it moves towards them progressively, beginning with a statement that gives more than a general idea, but which remains short of giving them in full detail. Thus, it serves as an index to the principles of faith and to the codes of Islam: *"But truly righteous is he who believes in God and the Last Day, and the angels and the Book and the Prophets; and gives his money, much as it is dear to him, to his kinsfolk, to the orphans, to the needy, to the traveller in need, and the beggars and for the freeing of slaves; who attends to his prayers and pays zakat; [and righteous are they] who remain true to their promises whenever they promise, and are patient in misfortune and adversity and in the time of peril. Such are those who have proved themselves to be true, and such are those who fear God."* (2: 177.)

Consider also how, when the rules of faith are outlined here, they are not given in their normal order which is followed on more than one occasion earlier in the surah. Here, the two ends are put together first, 'belief *in God and the Last Day*,' while the middle ones, 'belief in the angels, revelation and prophets', come later. This is because these are the medium through which the laws and rules are made known. Hence, they are kept to the last so that when they come together nothing intervenes to separate them. Moreover, the constituents of this medium are given in the right order, starting with the angels who bring down the revelations, followed by the Book which embodies the revelations, and finally the prophets who receive revelations. Now the surah goes on to outline the legislation that we have received through the prophets.

The Third Purpose of the Surah (Verses 178-283)

Having laid the foundation, the *surah* now begins the job of raising the structure. When the outer structure is firmly established, attention is paid to completing its internal parts. The surah has attended fully to purifying the faith, which is the essence of religion. Now it provides the details of the law, which give the religion its appearance. All doubts raised by critics have been dispelled and their arguments refuted. The task now is to illuminate the way for those who wish to follow it, and to make clear to them the purpose of the law. Attention so far has been given to clarifying the principles of faith; but now it turns to explaining the laws of Islam.

We have seen how the surah has prepared the way for this transition. It included a linking passage to relate the different parts of the discourse. If we were to cast a quick side glance, we will find that the final verse in this passage is the one quoted earlier, verse 177, which outlines the theoretical and practical aspects of righteousness. We also find that the aspect nearer to us is the practical one given in this verse in the form of a list of headings. It is now time to explain it in detail.

Righteousness and Patience in Adversity

In 106 verses we see a new type of meaning outlining the practical system to be followed by believers. It gives them details of what is required of them as duty, what is permissible and what is forbidden in different aspects of life, with respect to the individual, the family and the community. The surah may just start a topic, or it may discuss it in an answer to a question that has been put to the Prophet. It, thus, gives clear legislation with numerous points of detail.

It is, indeed, very wise to delay the work on the structure until its foundations have been firmly laid down, and to speak about details only after the fundamental concepts and rules have been completed. However, when we look carefully at these details and consider that they are bricks firmly held together, or a necklace with superbly arranged pearls, we discern a definite and wise purpose drawn in sharp relief as we compare the earlier summary and the forthcoming details.

It is now time to look at the main areas in this part. Verse 177 which summed up all aspects of righteousness concludes with a quality given special emphasis, as it is presented in three different forms. This quality is patience and it is shown here as necessary when facing misfortune or adversity and at times of real danger. Now that the surah begins to give the details, it takes up this very quality, with its three specified aspect, tackling them in reverse order to that mentioned in the outline. Thus, it speaks first about patience when facing danger, then patience in adversity and finally patience when facing misfortune. The same progressive pattern is followed when giving details of each of the qualities of righteousness: honouring promises and contracts, attending to prayers, payment of zakat, and also financial and physical sacrifice for God's cause. Let us now have a quick look at these details:

Patience in times of peril. This does not mean patience when one suffers injuries in war, for this is a negative aspect of patience. Nor is the main reference here to the type of patience required to inflict defeat on the enemy. This is definitely a positive type of patience, but it relies on physical strength. Islam, however, emphasises moral strength as being far more important. The Prophet says: "A truly strong person is not the one who physically overcome others. The truly strong is a person who maintains self control when angry." Likewise, God gives us here the most effective and superior example of patience, which is to remain in control in times of peril. This provides the best restraining mechanism against pursuing vengeance or killing opponents indiscriminately. This patience imposes a limit that must not be exceeded, which is to maintain fairness in retaliation (2: 178-179). As one thought calls up another, the discussion of people that have been killed leads to talking about those about to die. Thus, the topic concludes with the duty of one who is about to die to be kind to his relatives and to make a will in their favour. (2: 189-182.)

Patience in adversity. Here again God chooses the most difficult type of patience when facing hard times. This is superior to tolerating illness and pain patiently. It is to be patient when one suffers thirst and hunger willingly, only to obey God's orders. This is shown in the discussion of fasting (2: 183-187). The drift moves on from speaking about temporary abstention from taking lawful things to total and permanent abstention from the unlawful devouring of other people's property (2: 188).

Patience in misfortune. The same pattern is followed here. What the surah is talking about in this type is not the sort of enforced patience in poverty, or when one experiences a financial hardship or an unexpected crisis. It is referring to the patience needed on the basis of choice, when one makes a financial sacrifice, spending one's money to serve God's cause. The example the Qur'an gives here is of a dual nature, combining patience in both misfortune and adversity, combining physical and financial jihad; that is, pilgrimage (2: 189-202). It is, indeed, a three-pronged example, because it includes a reference to fighting the enemies of God, which involves patience in times of peril. (2: 190-195). Perhaps we should not forget to refer here to the easy passage through which the discussion progresses from talking about fasting to talking about pilgrimage. This is achieved through the references to the new moons, which God has defined as indicators of the periods of both fasting and pilgrimage. (2: 190.)

Perhaps it is appropriate to take a short pause here, to dwell on a particular aspect of the flow of topics in the Qur'an as we have here a vivid example of it. When pilgrimage is mentioned the first time, it is not followed immediately by a detailed outline of its rules and regulations. In fact, 6 verses, 190-195, separate the first mention of pilgrimage and the outline of its regulations. These verses give detailed rules concerning jihad, both physical and financial, in the case of a war with the enemies of Islam.

An ignorant person may claim that this separation is odd. However, anyone who is aware of the history of Islam and the reasons leading to the revelation of various verses will know that this gap serves an important purpose and occurs in its rightful position. To start with, there is a time link between the legislation requiring Muslims to offer the pilgrimage and the events at al-Hudaibiyah, near Makkah, when the Prophet and his Companions were forcibly prevented from entering Makkah to offer the ᶜumrah. This eventually led to the signing of a peace agreement known as the al-Hudaibiyah treaty in the 6th year of the Islamic calendar. What is more important is the fact that the performance of the rituals of ᶜumrah at that time remained an unfulfilled intention, frustrating a long entertained hope. The Muslims were held back and prevented from offering their worship at the Kaᶜbah. They were keen to strike hard at their enemies, but God commanded them not to be the ones to start fighting, and not to fight their enemies in the vicinity of the Sacred Mosque, except those who fight them in it. They submitted to God's orders and went back home awaiting the fulfilment of God's promise.

In the same way, let the reader or the listener here wait and consider this intervening passage before he learns the details of the pilgrimage, which he is eager to know. This parallels the waiting of those Muslims who turned back to Madinah when they were most eager to go to Makkah, postponing that visit for a year. Thus, these intervening verses serve as a permanent commemoration of those events in the early history of Islam. The Qur'an provides a clear view of all the facts. Some of these we learn as they are mentioned specifically and in detail. Others we get to know implicitly through the style and order of discussion. This passage, thus, provides a practical example of a student's patience when his teacher is giving his lesson. The student does not hasten to interrupt him with his questions. He waits until the teacher decides to discuss the relevant point. We do not have to wait long for the rules and regulations concerning the pilgrimage and the ʿ*umrah* for these are shortly given in detail. They are awaited most eagerly, like a thirsty person waits for his cool drink. (2: 196-203.) When this is concluded, the first set of legislation is completed, dealing with all aspects of patience in misfortune, adversity and in the face of danger.

A relaxing passage (Verses 204-214)

In His wisdom and kindness, God does not take us straight up to the next stage. He gives us a pause for relaxation, which reinforces our will to obey His orders. He gives us here a general admonition which consolidates what has already been achieved and eases us into what is yet to come. This general admonition comes in the most fitting place, with a direct link to the special reminder with which the discussion of pilgrimage is concluded. This reminder divides people, with respect to their hopes and aspirations, into two types: those who pursue nothing but the comforts and pleasures of this worldly life, paying little or no attention to the Hereafter, and those whose aim is happiness in the life to come without forgetting the needs of this present life, (2: 200-202). Now we see the general admonition dividing people into two broad groups: those who pursue only their own interests, even though that means ruining other people's lives and spreading corruption in the land, and those who seek God's pleasure, ready to sacrifice their lives for that, (2: 204-207).

After this division, the surah gives a piece of sincere advice to the believers to purge their hearts and souls of any trace of personal desire and to submit themselves completely to God, drawing no distinction between one set of His orders and another. It warns them against straying away from the path God has marked for them to follow. It encourages them to remain patient whatever they may have to face of misfortune or adversity, setting for them examples from earlier communities. (2: 208-214.)

To Honour Promises and Covenants

This general reminder concludes the relaxing passage. Now the surah moves to the second set of laws which comprise more details of the practical manifestation of the second quality of righteousness mentioned in general terms in verse 177. This quality is to be true to one's commitments and to honour one's promises and pledges. The surah chooses the contract most deserving of being honoured; that is, marriage and all that it entails of establishing a family, and the rights of the family members. The family is the first environment where a person receives his or her training to deal well with others and to purge oneself of selfishness. Besides, when matters are set right in the small social set up of the family, they are likely to be set right in the larger set up of a local, and then a national, community.

How will the surah make its progress to this second set of details? Will it turn suddenly to discuss the details of complicated domestic issues? Here the surah has an edifying purpose and it does not serve that purpose to lay down a host of instructions without preparing us for what is to come. In fact, the surah makes its route to outlining them easily, using a platform of questions and answers. The first of these questions relate to the earlier legislation governing spending and jihad, (2: 215-218), while the last are closely linked to legislation still to come, such as the regulations concerning orphans and how to manage their affairs, conditions for accepting a proposal of marriage, and restrictions on marital relationship. (2: 220-222.)

Here, we need to reflect seriously on this fine and detailed pattern and ask how its various pieces have all been slotted into place. How could this have happened without the events providing its subject matter all materialising, or if some of them failed to take place? Alternatively, what if they had all taken place but without raising the relevant questions in people's minds? We see here destiny serving the setting order of the Qur'an. It first ensures that events take place in a particular way to provide the subject matter to be discussed, then raises questions in people's minds and from these they formulate their requests for instruction. All that is left for us to do is to declare our belief that the One who controls time and its events is indeed the One who reveals the Qur'an. *"His is all creation and all command. Hallowed be God, the Lord of all the worlds."* (7: 54.)

This easy progress leads to the discussion of the central points in the second set of legislation, leaving no gap and resorting to no sudden departure. Verses 223-237 provide a complete code of conduct for family life. This comes in two parts: the first deals with family matters when the family is together, (2: 223-232), while the second provides the rules to deal with the break up of family life, (2: 233-237).

Consider, if you will, this set of rules given in the surah, and study the events leading to its revelation. You will find that each issue referred to in these verses provides a verdict on a particular event that has no relation or bearing on the other events. Now look carefully at the style employed here to outline these rules and regulations and try hard to find in it any trace of disjointed speech, or determine whether there is any point where two different parts are joined or welded together. All your attempts in this regard will be in vain. You will only find here a single whole, made up of a single fabric, although numerous elements are used in its manufacture.

The Semantic Design of the Longest *Surah*

Let us consider the line of discussion. It begins first with laying the foundation, emphasising the right to sexual relations within marriage, (2: 223). It follows this with an order to refrain from making any oaths to restrict such sacred rights, whether the oath entails the withholding of kindness from anyone who is entitled to it, or to severing a bond which God wants to be maintained, (2: 224-225). It then goes on to lay down rules covering a certain part of this principle relating to marital life. That is, the rules in the case of a man who swears not to touch his wife, (2: 226-227). This leads directly to the rules governing divorce and what rights and duties apply after divorce, (the verses beginning with 2: 238).

If you look now with admiration at this logical flow treating complex issues that were widely separate to start with, raised by uncoordinated events, I will point out to you a particle which illustrates the perfect design that brings together all these divergent elements making of them a complete and coherent whole. This is the conjunction that facilitates the progress from the rules on the case of swearing not to touch one's wife to the rules of divorce. *"Those who take an oath that they will not approach their wives shall have four months of grace. Then, if they go back on their oaths, God is much-forgiving, merciful. And if they are resolved on divorce, [let them remember that] God hears all and knows all. Divorced women shall wait...."* (2: 226-8.)

Consider how the rule on swearing not to approach one's wife has been phrased in such a way that prepares us for tempestuous situations that could lead to divorce. Thus, when divorce is discussed in detail immediately afterwards, the discussion flows naturally and falls perfectly into place. In fact, the tail of the first rule serves as an opening leading to the next point. When the rules on divorce begin they are felt to be a natural progression. Indeed, the whole discussion sounds as the treatment of a single topic with no gap between its parts.

Had the Qur'an been the work of Muhammad, who could have informed him in advance that he would be one day asked to provide detailed rules on divorce? Who could have told him that he would then be able to give a detailed answer which was also joined to the rules on vowing not to touch one's wife. How could he have known that the proper flow of speech would necessitate that these latter rules, which he was outlining earlier, should be so arranged that they refer in the final instance to the possibility of divorce in order to fit with the answers he had yet to give to questions which would be asked of him later? How could he have known in advance that this would be the only way to join the rules together when they were to be outlined and explained? Such knowledge of future events belongs to no human being. It is the preserve of the One who knows everything that is present or hidden, the One who has shaped every creature and guided them all on their respective courses.

The *surah* moves on along its new course, giving details of the legislation on divorce and all that it entails: a waiting period, re-marriage of divorcees, *khul^c* or the termination of marriage at the wife's request, breast-feeding by divorced mothers or by wet nurses, marriage proposals, dowries, the right of a divorced woman to compensation, etc. This second set takes us up to verse 237.

The third set is presented in verses 238-274, and begins with the instruction, "*Attend regularly to your prayers, particularly the middle prayer.*" But how is this switch from the second to the third set of rules achieved?

We find here a complete contrast with the earlier switch from the first to the second set of rules. There the transition is made so easy, providing ample time for relaxation. Here the opposite is true. The transition is made so suddenly that one may think it an abrupt departure made in the interests of brevity. But that is only a superficial view. A more comprehensive view of the progress of discussion, however, one following the line determined in verse 177 outlining the qualities of righteousness, shows a totally different picture. The surah has now covered two thirds of the qualities outlined, beginning with the discussion of patience in misfortune, adversity and in times of peril, then moving to honouring promises and commitments. It is now time to speak about the last third which includes such elements as prayer, zakat, and making financial sacrifices for God's cause. This discussion comes here at its fitting place in accordance with the outline made in the earlier verse.

An Abrupt or a Prepared Switch?

Someone may yet say that the transition remains abrupt, unprepared. The fact is that it is not so. There has been proper and sufficient preparation at the conclusion of the final verse in the previous section. That conclusion may be rendered in translation as follows: "*To forgo what is due to you [of specified dowry] is closer to being righteous. Do not forget to act benevolently to one another. Truly, God sees all that you do.*" (2: 237.) This conclusion serves as a perfect passageway placed at the right spot, after the long and detailed discussion of rights and duties within the family home. This passageway leads us from the atmosphere of conflict and persistent demands to that of benevolence and forgoing one's rights. It, thus, takes us a step higher on the virtue ladder, and prepares us to be elevated to an even higher level.

Consider the instruction: "*Do not forget to act benevolently to one another.*" Every letter here suggests that these are the words of a dear one who is departing after having stayed with us for a while to arbitrate in our disputes. He is now folding his book of rules in order to turn to something more important. As he folds it, he advises us to stop bickering over such trivial details and to sort them out on the basis of righteousness and benevolence. This is far more suitable and more superior to strict justice and insisting on taking one's full rights. He further tells us to turn to far more important matters which need our greater resolve and to place these in their rightful place at the top of our preoccupations. He is just telling us: you have had enough about the rights of spouses and offspring. It is time to discuss your duties towards God and your community. Attend to your prayers; spend your money for God's sake and fight to serve His cause.

It is timely to consider whether the reference to prayer made here is a major and independent issue or merely part of a larger issue. To answer this point properly we need to refer back to the verse that outlined aspects of righteousness (2: 177) and to consider how these are treated in subsequent verses, right up to the final part of the surah. We need to compare how much care each aspect is given in this glorious Qur'an.

A proper look at these parts will show us that the two qualities of spending one's money and exerting one's efforts to serve God's cause, i.e. jihad, are repeatedly highlighted at the opening and at different junctures, when the surah speaks of general matters and detailed ones. Such frequent emphasis gives a clear indication that it is the prime objective of legislation in this surah. In light of this, if we reflect on the social environment where these revelations took place and the events leading to them, and if we picture in our minds the community to which such legislation was sent down, we paint a picture of a camp preparing for a struggle requiring financial and physical sacrifice. At the head of this camp we find an alert and caring leader, who takes notice of every little detail of the affairs of his soldiers, whether personal or general. He gives them advice and issues orders concerning all such matters. Whenever he finishes with incidental or temporary matters, his discourse turns back to their central mission.

When we put this military picture in front of our eyes, we are not surprised that jihad emerges now as the principal topic after the legislation on family matters has been completed. In fact, it has never been far from the drift of the discussion. If the surah now returns to it and gives it full attention, this is only natural. It continues what has already been there from the start. There is no need to justify raising it anew.

But what are we saying? And why are we referring to jihad when the surah is about to discuss prayer and the waiting period of a widow? Well, in fact, the surah does now concentrate on jihad. The reference to prayer and other matters is addressed to fighters for God's cause in this particular capacity. It addresses problems raised by the very condition of jihad, before giving them the express order to fight for God's cause.

The Semantic Design of the Longest *Surah*

The first problem concerns prayer at a time of war. Does jihad and fighting constitute a concession exempting Muslims from the duty of prayer or at least enabling them to postpone it? The answer given in the Qur'an is that no exemption from, or delay of, prayer is permitted in peace or war, in times of security or fear: "*Attend regularly to your prayer, particularly the middle prayer.*" (2: 238). The only concession in time of fear relates to the method and form of offering prayer: "*If you are in fear, pray walking or riding. When you are again secure, remember God since He has taught you what you did not know.*" (2: 239.)

As we know, prayer enhances moral strength and serves as an important element that is essential for the achievement of victory. Hence, it is only wise that those who are preparing for jihad should tap its beneficial moral before they are given the express order to fight. At the same time, prayer purges the worshipper's soul of ill manners and unbecoming traits such as being mean and stingy. God describes man as follows: "*When good fortune comes to him [i.e. man], he selfishly withholds it [from others]. Not so, however, those who attend properly to their prayers.*" (70: 21-22.) Thus, it is only right that this order should come here to reinforce the earlier advice on showing benevolence in all our dealings.

Thus, the talk about prayer here has a dual benefit: it serves as a cure and spiritual nutrition at the same time. It looks both backwards and forwards. We may even say that it has a triple benefit, because when it looks back, it does not only look at the preceding verse only; it also looks at the earlier verse that summed up righteousness to give more details on this aspect.

When you appreciate the finer elements of style which enable the easy flow from one purpose to another, and the fine structure which ensures perfect harmony between earlier and later points and topics, you are certain that no abrupt departure occurs as the surah picks up the point on prayer. However, when we compare the gentle and relaxed transition from the first to the second sections with the quick and sudden transition made here, we may think that this is not sufficiently prepared. In fact, a jerk is felt here at the sudden turn imposed. Yet this rapid move is intended, not least because it contributes to the instruction of the believers. The sudden turn shows what a true believer's attitude should be when he or she hears the call to attend to their spiritual duty while they are totally absorbed with life's affairs. Thus, the surah practically tells us that believers do not require much struggle in order to elevate themselves above their preoccupations with family and children. They can always lift themselves immediately in order to attend to their superior duty. In this they say to the whole world, 'Leave us alone; we want to offer our worship.' This is, indeed, the characteristic of believers as the Qur'an describes them: *"They are impelled to rise from their beds [at night] to call out on their Lord in fear and hope."* (32: 16.)

Striving for God's Cause

Jihad is the main theme in the next part of the surah. A soldier in war is preoccupied with two worries at least. He first worries about what may happen to him and his fellow fighters and the risks of death and defeat they face, then he worries about his family and dependants who may suffer if he were killed. Hence, the surah proceeds immediately to reassure him about both anxieties. As far as his wife is concerned, God enjoins that when a woman is widowed, she is to stay for a complete year in his home. Even a divorced wife has the right to be generously treated and this right may not be forgotten. He, thus, may be reassured on this count, (2: 240-242). As for his concern about death, Muslims should know that he who does not mind death may have a long life to enjoy: *"Have you reflected on [the case of] those who left their homes in their thousands for fear of death? God said to them, 'Die,' and later He brought them back to life?"* (2: 243). As for worry about defeat, let all believers learn that victory is granted by God: *"How often has a small host triumphed over a large host by God's grace."* (2: 249.) This is, indeed, the standard practice in the case of God's messengers, (2: 246-253).

The Semantic Design of the Longest *Surah*

Thus, all fears are dispelled once the fighters are equipped with the moral support of God-consciousness. They are now ready to receive His supreme order, to fight for His cause, sacrificing their property and their lives, (2: 244-245). Historical examples are given in order to strengthen them in times of peril and to enhance their hopes of victory, (2: 246-253). It should be noted that the Qur'anic style here differs from its normal educational method, when the conclusion comes at the end of the line. Here, the premises are shown in a circle and the result falls at the centre of that circle. The order to fight for God's cause, (2: 244), is given strong support at both sides, and the support is shown in general terms at first and in full detail at the end. But this exceptional treatment is not peculiar to this instance in the Qur'an. There are several other examples of it in God's book.

Perhaps we should add here that jihad is of two types: one involving personal and self sacrifice and the other involving financial sacrifice. The latter is not limited to financing the war effort only. It includes readily giving money to anything that improves the community's situation, strengthens the power of the Islamic state and protects Islam and Muslims.

Personal sacrifice for God's cause was first identified in a short verse, (2: 244) and then elaborated upon in several verses, (2: 246-253). Financial sacrifice as an aspect of jihad is also briefly mentioned in a short verse, (2: 255), so it is only right that it should be addressed in detail in several others. As this takes place, the treatment starts in a rather strong way, (2: 254-260). These verses give a stern warning to miserly people, reminding them of the day when no one can make an offering to ensure one's happiness, and when no friend or intercessor is of any help. This meaning is reinforced so as to remove any lingering doubt in the mind of anyone who still hopes to be saved through the intercession or the influence of anyone other than God, and to drive home the message concerning the Day of Judgement. The aim here is to ensure that spending one's money to further God's cause is motivated only by pure faith, seeking no reward from anyone other than God. Then the treatment of financial sacrifice in jihad takes a much softer line, (2: 261), before it takes an educative aspect showing the good manners that must be observed when spending for God's cause, (2: 262-274).

The discussion then moves on from talking about sacrifice, which is the noblest social virtue, to discussing fully the vice of greed and self-aggrandisement, which is at the opposite end of the social scale. It highlights the most repugnant form of human transaction, usury, which seeks to exploit the needs of the weak and the deprived, while the rich exact a price for the help they provide, (2: 275-279). That the two are juxtaposed in this way highlights the contrast between them for any person with a conscience.

In between these two contrasting types of dealing, the Qur'an establishes the fair criterion, giving the creditor the right to claim his principal amount in full, writing nothing off: "*You shall commit no wrong, nor suffer any wrong yourselves.*" (2: 279). However, the Qur'an warns us that we should not use this right against people going through hardship. It instructs us to take one of two benevolent measures: either to delay one's loan until the debtor's circumstances have eased up or to forgo the loan completely, which is a much better course to follow: "*Should you give free will offerings, it would be for your own good, if you but knew it.*", (2: 289-281).

The prominent aspect in this Qur'anic legislation is one of content and generosity, which may impart a sense of complacency concerning money. It may also encourage a lax attitude about investing money to ensure its increase. Hence the surah includes two verses, the first of which is the longest in the Qur'an, which discuss credits and pledges, (2: 282-283). These two verses dispel any such false impressions and lay down for the believers the most perfect code of conduct in recording, documenting and certifying financial rights and obligations. This is preparatory to spending money only for beneficial purposes. When there is nothing available to document a transaction, and one party is obliged to place his trust in the other's honesty, a clear instruction is given: "*If you trust one another, let him who is trusted fulfil his trust, and let him fear God, his Lord.*". (2: 283.)

Thus, the practical part of the surah is concluded with this perfect rule, basic to all honourable dealings: the rule of honesty and the fulfilment of trust. May God grant us all the virtues of being honest and trustworthy.

A Higher Level than Faith

The fourth purpose of the surah is tackled in one verse only, verse 284. In the verse preceding this, the section giving detailed legislation was concluded at the point determined for it by God. It included all legislation He has wished to include in this surah. Thus, the second part of the religious truth, which is the practical part, was completed. The solid foundation of its first part, i.e. faith itself, has already been laid down, beginning with verse 122. This means that the surah has by now completed its discussion of the fundamentals of faith and Islamic legislation. Is there anything left in the structure of religion apart from these pillars?

Yes indeed. What is left is its highest summit and most perfect adornment. When we have discussed faith and the religion of Islam, what remains is to bring it all to perfection, or to use the Islamic term, *iḥsān*. This quality was explained by God's Messenger, (peace be upon him). He defines it as watching God in all our affairs, feeling that He is seeing us in public and private, and being prepared for the event when He will put us to account even for what we entertain in our hearts and for our innermost thoughts. This is far from easy. Its full achievement is beyond every Muslim, indeed beyond every believer. Among the God-fearing only the elite of the elite come near it. Perhaps because of its rarity in practice and its great value, God describes this inimitable jewel in this single verse which serves as the crown for the whole surah: *"Whether you make known what is in your minds or conceal it, God will bring you to account for it."* (2: 284.)

Now we come to the conclusion of the surah, summed up in the two final verses, (2: 285-286). Having discussed the pillars of religion and explained all its constituent elements: faith, submission or Islam, and perfection, what is left is to finish the discussion and declare it closed. Let us consider now how this is done.

Remember the five opening verses and consider how that opening corresponds to the present conclusion. In fact, the opening and the conclusion tie up together to form a perfect siege demarcating the boundaries of the surah and making of it a single structure, perfectly raised and with clear boundaries. This is indeed the linguistic meaning of the term surah, which is used in Arabic only to refer to the units of the Qur'an. The term is derived from a root that signifies something with a fence or a solid line separating it from others.

The opening of the surah constituted a generous promise to those who believe in it and who implement its orders. These are certain to be properly guided and are certain to prosper. Our expectations are now raised to try to find out the response to this promise. We need to know whether anyone has believed in it and followed its guidance. If so, we also expect to learn about the reward of those who have listened to its message and followed it.

This is, indeed, the conclusion of the surah. It is composed of 1) an announcement of the success of its message: *"The Messenger believes in what has been revealed to him by his Lord, and so do the believers... And they say, 'We hear and we obey.'"* (2: 285). 2) A fulfilment of its promise to every soul that has done its best in following its guidance: *"To its credit shall be whatever good it does and against it whatever evil it does."* (2: 286) 3) Leaving the door of hope wide open for those who follow guidance. They raise their hands in an earnest prayer: *"Our Lord, do not take us to task if we forget or lapse into error. Our Lord, do not lay on us a burden such as that which You laid on those before us. Our Lord, do not burden us with what we do not have the strength to bear. Pardon us, forgive us our sins, and have mercy on us. You alone are our Lord Supreme: grant us, then, victory over the unbelievers."* (2: 286.)

Thus the surah concludes. Do we discern its unity despite its length? Do we realise how its lines converge to complete its picture? Indeed, its bricks are firmly put in place without any sealant to join them together. Its dome is raised without any pillars to support it. Its head, body and limbs are joined together to give the most perfect living shape. Every atom is perfectly placed in its cell, every cell in its organ, every organ in its system and every system in its body: each one declares that it takes its assigned position in accordance with a well defined plan, charted by the One who purifies souls, enlightens minds and guides spirits. If this surah was arranged after its revelation had been completed, grouping its parts together in this way would have been a miracle. What can we say when we realise that every passage of it, like every passage in every other surah, was placed in its position right at the time of its revelation. In fact, a position was reserved for every subsequent passage, awaiting its revelation. It is, indeed, a true fact that the passages that had not yet been revealed were assigned their final positions long before their revelation. What is more is that alone among the surahs revealed in separate passages, the actual position of each passage in this surah was defined nine years before its revelation commenced. That was the length of time it took for all its parts to be revealed.

The Qur'an is miraculous not only in its powerful style, method of education and its true prophesies, but also in its legislation which is appropriate for all generations. Indeed, it is even more miraculous with all the scientific facts it mentions relating to the human soul and the universe. However, the arrangement of its verses in the way we have seen is the miracle that transcends all miracles.

www.ingramcontent.com/pod-product-compliance
Lightning Source LLC
LaVergne TN
LVHW040048080526
838202LV00045B/3545